IMPROVING STUDENT BEHAVIOR

Essays on Classroom Management and Motivation

Thomas R. McDaniel

UNIVERSITY
PRESS OF
AMERICA

LANHAM • NEW YORK • LONDON

Copyright © 1987 by

University Press of America,® Inc.

4720 Boston Way
Lanham, MD 20706

3 Henrietta Street
London WC2E 8LU England

British Cataloging in Publication Information Available

Library of Congress Cataloging in Publication Data

McDaniel, Thomas R.
   Improving student behavior.

   Includes bibliographies.
   1. School discipline—United States.   2. Classroom
management—United States.   3. Motivation in education.
   I. Title.
   LB3012.M38   1987   371.1'024   86-28228
   ISBN 0-8191-6064-4 (alk. paper)
   ISBN 0-8191-6065-2 (pbk. : alk. paper)

All University Press of America books are produced on acid-free
paper which exceeds the minimum standards set by the National
Historical Publication and Records Commission.

DEDICATION

For John and Jean, Sally and Al, Susan and Ned:
Siblings and Siblings-in-law. Over the years
their behavior **has** improved.

ACKNOWLEDGMENTS

I am indebted to many people for their assistance in publishing this book of essays on classroom management and motivation. I am grateful to James Lyons and Helen Hudson of University Press of America for their editorial support and guidance. I appreciate the typing and proofreading help I have received from Gwyn Lamm, Clara DeLamar, and Martha Hartley. Converse College has provided financial support, and I am especially grateful to the Kenan Fund for its support of Faculty Research and Development at this College. As always, I appreciate the ideas and criticisms offered by my students at Converse. They are a wonderful testing ground for my educational theories and strategies. And thanks to Nan, Robb, and Katy--always my best critics and teachers.

CREDITS

The articles in this volume, all written by Thomas R. McDaniel, are reprinted with the permission of the following publishers:

Phi Delta Kappan for "Exploring Alternatives to Punishment: Keys to Effective Discipline" (vol. 61, no. 7, March, 1980); "A Primer on Motivation: Principles Old and New" (vol. 66, no. 1, September, 1984); "A Primer on Classroom Discipline: Principles Old and New" (vol. 68, no. 1, September 1986).

The Clearing House for "Corporal Punishment and Teacher Liability: Questions Teachers Ask" (vol. 54, no. 1, September, 1980); "How to Be A More Effective Authoritarian" (vol. 55, no. 6, February, 1982); "The Ten Commandments of Motivation" (vol. 59, no. 1, September, 1985); "School Discipline in Perspective" (vol. 59, no. 8, April, 1986). "Practicing Positive Reinforcement: Ten Behavior Management Techniques" (future issue).

Teaching for Excellence for "Improving Student Behavior Through Effective Language Techniques" (vol. v, No. 3, November, 1985).

Childhood Education for "Identifying Discipline Problems: A Self-Evaluation Exercise" (vol. 57, no. 4, March/April, 1981). Reprinted by permission of Thomas R. McDaniel and the Association for Childhood Education International, 11141 Georgia Avenue, Wheaton, Md 20902. Copyright 1981 by the Association.

Early Years for "Discipline--Just Another One of the Basics" (vol. x, no. 2, October, 1979). Reprinted with the permission of the publisher, Allen Raymond, Inc., Darien, Ct 06820. This article is a retitled and revised version of "So You Want Good Classroom Behavior? Don't Preach It--Teach It!"

Educational Leadership for "Developing the Skills of Humanistic Discipline" (vol. 41, no. 8, May, 1984). Reprinted with permission of the Association for Supervision and Curriculum Development. Copyright (c) 1984 by the Association for Supervision and Curriculum Development.

Orbit: Ideas About Teaching and Learning for "'Well Begun is Half Done': A School-Wide Project for Better Discipline" (vol. 13, no. 1, February, 1982).

American Secondary Education for "'A Stitch in Time': Principles of Preventive Discipline" (vol. 9, no. 2, June, 1979).

The Educational Forum for "Power in the Classroom" (vol. XLVI, no. 1, Fall, 1981).

TABLE OF CONTENTS

x

INTRODUCTION

Few topics are of greater interest--to educators **and** the public--than school discipline. This present volume of essays looks at school discipline from a variety of perspectives but always with the optimism of the author: we **can** improve student behavior. Improving student behavior in public school classrooms will require major efforts by educators and the public, and it will require careful consideration of the problems teachers encounter daily. But progress is possible.

Part I of this volume examines theoretical issues in managing and motivating students. What is the role of teacher education in preparing new teachers and assisting experienced ones as they deal with discipline? What is the place of "power" in the classroom and how might power be best used to develop an effective model of school discipline? Does punishment work--or must we find alternative practices of management and motivation? What legal issues should teachers be sensitive to if they employ corporal punishment? What exactly **is** a "discipline problem"? Those who can answer such questions with confidence and clarity are well on their way to understanding the dynamics of discipline in our public school classrooms.

Part II of this volume moves from theory to practice. Here the questions addressed revolve around strategies that derive **from** theories--traditional, behavioral, humanistic--and culminate in a variety of techniques that educators can use to improve student behavior. Teachers can be more effective in communicating their authority if they know how to use rules, consequences, and classroom structure. They can prevent many management problems from occurring if they know how to predict them and prepare for them. They can **teach** students how to behave more appropriately and can use language more effectively to respond to certain kinds of behavioral problems. And, surely, teachers can refine techniques of motivation and skills of humanistic discipline to increase their pedagogical power in the classroom. Those who can use strategies skillfully and humanely can become masters in the art of discipline.

Part III of this volume synthesizes principles and practices of the art of discipline in two "primers."

The first primer outlines ten major principles of management and suggests specific practices that should follow each principle. The second primer identifies five major principles of motivation and suggests a variety of techniques that teachers might use to put each principle to work in the classroom. Both primers include an inventory by which teachers can rate their practices.

Improving Student Behavior provides a hopeful view of the number one issue in public education: school discipline. It provides no panacea or simple prescription but, rather, suggests that teachers can--within their own philosophical and pedagogical frame-works--improve student behavior by improving their own ability to manage and motivate today's youth.

PART I

THEORIES: An Eclectic Model of Discipline

SCHOOL DISCIPLINE IN PERSPECTIVE

In September 1985, the 17th annual Gallup Poll of the public's attitudes toward public schools indicated once again--for the 16th time--that discipline is perceived as the number one problem in American education. Seven out of ten respondents said the lack of discipline was "fairly serious" to "very serious." The 1986 poll listed discipline second--right below drugs. Are the public schools of this nation on the brink of anarchy?

Item: A popular Greenville, South Carolina, social studies teacher and coach is stabbed to death in his classroom by a mentally disturbed female student in the fall of 1981.

Item: In a 1975 Senate subcommittee report, Senator Birch Bayh said that violence and vandalism in the nation's schools amounted yearly to more than one-half billion dollars in damage, 100 murders, 12,000 armed robberies, and over 200,000 assaults on teachers and students. In the decade since, no appreciable decline in this violence is evident.

Item: One survey of teachers in Chicago found 56.6 percent of 5,500 respondents claiming physical and/or mental illness as a direct result of their jobs. So-called "teacher burnout," sometimes referred to as battle fatigue or combat neurosis, is most frequently attributed to stress resulting from student harassment, apathy, and disrespect.

Item: A cartoon in a professional education journal shows a principal reporting to his faculty. He says, "The results of our recent faculty instructional needs assessment are as follows: 18 of you desire full-time security guards, 12 requested closed-circuit video surveillance, 8 want metal detectors, 6 need attack guards, and one asked for a workshop on teaching map skills."

We are numbed by an unrelenting succession of such items in the press, professional journals, and parlor gossip. But we should keep the school discipline problem in proper perspective.

Problems

In the first place, we ought to remember that the public schools reflect the problems and changes in the

3

society at large. This is not to say that schools are blameless; it is to say that schools today are serving large numbers of children who come from broken homes (does anyone need to be reminded of current divorce rates?), from diverse cultures (including the "new immigrants," both legal and illegal), and from populations not previously served in those public schools (e.g., the handicapped). Although the public schools should serve **all** of the public, the present student population is simply more difficult to deal with because it **is** diverse.

In the second place, youngsters today live with more freedom and independence than ever before. Some of this freedom has come by parental default--"latch key" children, for example, are quite common in our society--and some has been created by the success of materialism. Not everyone has "benefited" from this generation's economic prosperity, of course, but many students have not learned the values of discipline--hard work, sacrifice, perseverance, and responsibility. In an important sense, these children have been deprived by an easy life of charge cards, luxury, and instant gratification. Many high school students drive to school in better cars than teachers can afford. Why should such students think they should respect and obey teachers?

In the third place, we ought to recognize that the diverse population of contemporary public school students, often cut loose from traditional moorings of discipline and respect for authority, are confronted with a variety of influences that undermine good order in the schools. Television shortens attention spans, contributes to restlessness, and (ironically) tends to make youngsters passive. By the age of 18, the average child will have spent 45 percent more time watching television than attending school and will have witnessed 15,000 TV "deaths." Drugs affect behavior too. By 1981 figures, one in fourteen seniors uses marijuana daily, three in ten use amphetamines, and one in four reports "binge" drinking.

It is easy to find culprits in the school discipline dilemma: parents who do not instill respect for authority in their children; children who do not see the value in schools; schools that are lax in enforcing rules and codes. I would place special responsibility on colleges and universities that prepare teachers to do a better job in helping teachers deal with discipline.

4

Solutions

Unfortunately, teacher education programs have given relatively little attention to the discipline dilemma. Too often we have dealt in cliches and bromides: (a) Don't smile until Christmas; (2) Be firm but gentle, friendly but aloof; (c) If your curriculum is first-rate, students will want to behave. We simply must do more for teachers and schools.

We can make school discipline a higher priority in research and in textbooks. As Edward Wynne notes, "Discipline is not ignored as a topic, but it is apparently not a matter of high concern" (1981, p. 380). Surely, those of us who study and write about education can devote more time and effort to finding solutions to the discipline dilemma. What **is** good discipline anyway? The public (according to the recent Gallup Poll) tends to think of generalities here--obeying rules and regulations, authority and control by teachers, student respect for teachers--but research should subject all of the significant factors to intense scrutiny. Whatever researchers find out about what promotes "good" discipline must then be made a prominent feature of texts used by prospective teachers. Many effective discipline techniques are already available but are not widely known or practiced by teachers: soft reprimands, "low profile" strategies, behavioral clinics, TET, logical consequences, "three dimensional" discipline, developmental discipline, social contracts, etc.

We can do more for schools by providing better in-service programs for veteran teachers. College and university education professors must be able to help teachers where they are. This means rolling up our sleeves and getting into schools where discipline problems are especially severe. The best approach is to provide school-wide training in a number of approaches to good discipline. Daniel Duke's **Systematic Management Plan for School Discipline** (1980), Lee Canter's **Assertive Discipline** (1976, 1979, 1981, 1982), and Phi Delta Kappa's **Handbook for Developing Schools with Good Discipline** (Wayson et al., 1982) are three examples of school-wide approaches to better discipline. Cracking down, reinstituting corporal punishment, security guards--these measures deal only with the symptoms of discipline and probably make things worse. I think we need to give schools workable programs that treat discipline as an **educational** problem, not merely as a **management** problem. Schools and teachers should help students learn how to govern their own behavior.

Finally we can do more to keep the public informed of our progress and perceptions. School discipline problems are often blown out of proportion. For example, in one survey of nearly 1300 superintendents across the nation, discipline was rated as only 13th among 18 problems they faced in public schools. There are **many** schools where discipline problems are rare and incidents are minor. We ought to remember that the adult generation has always bemoaned the sad state of discipline in the young. Consider this assessment:

> The children now love luxury; they show disrespect for elders and love chatter in place of exercise. Children are now tyrants, not the servants, of their households. . . . They contradict their parents, chatter before company, gobble up dainties at the table, cross their legs and tyrannize over their teacher.

This is from Socrates, circa 400 B.C. I think the discipline problem is a real one, but it is not as bad nor as new as we sometimes believe.

REFERENCES

Canter, L., & Canter, M. 1976. **Assertive discipline: A take charge approach for today's educator.** Los Angeles: Canter and Associates, Inc.

Canter, L., & Canter, M. 1979. **Assertive discipline: Competency-based resource materials and guidelines.** Los Angeles: Canter and Associates, Inc.

Canter, L., & Canter, M. 1981. **Assertive discipline: Follow-up guide.** Los Angeles: Canter and Associates, Inc.

Canter, L., & Canter, M. 1982. **Assertive discipline for parents.** Los Angeles: Canter and Associates, Inc.

Duke, D. L. & Meckel, A. M. 1980. **Managing student behavior problems.** New York: Teachers College Press.

Wayson, W. W., et al. 1982. **Handbook for developing schools with good discipline.** Bloomington, IN: Phi Delta Kappa.

Wynne, E. 1981, January. Looking at good schools. **Phi Delta Kappan,** p. 380.

POWER IN THE CLASSROOM

One of the major issues in education today is "the discipline problem." Statistics on school crime, vandalism, and violence are astounding.[1] The public puts such emphasis on good school discipline that its absence is cited as the number one problem in American education today.[2] Classroom control is a major concern of most teachers too, and a spate of manuals and texts has appeared in the last decade to tell teachers how to survive, cope, and maintain sanity in the classroom.[3] More teachers lose their jobs for inability to manage classrooms than for any other single reason. The stress that is generated by tension between teachers and students has created a syndrome that has been accorded its own label now--"teacher burnout."[4]

In the face of the school's discipline dilemma, the response of school boards and educators has been to crack down on offenders, beef-up police measures in schools, reinstitute corporal and other forms of punishment, and back-up disciplining teachers with strong administrative support. The assumption seems to be that problems of classroom discipline can best be solved by giving teachers and administrators more power over student behavior. Will a return to the traditional, punishment-oriented, and authoritarian approach to discipline solve the discipline problem in American schools? Does punishment work? Will giving more control over student behavior to teachers, administrators, and school boards improve education? These are loaded questions, of course, since the terms **solve**, **work**, and **improve** have varying definitions. I want to examine the discipline dilemma, and selected approaches to it in the classroom, from an analytical point of view in an attempt to evaluate some assumptions about the ends and means of education as they relate to this particular issue. At the heart of my analysis of school discipline is the concept of **power**.[5]

The Authoritarian Approach

One approach to school discipline, briefly outlined above, is advocated by a large number of educators and citizens. Those who call for quick and stern retribution for deviant behavior, violation of rules, and lack of obedience to established social norms employ an approach that is basically authoritarian in nature. Authoritarians share a general set of attitudes and beliefs about education and discipline:

7

. Power resides in the institution of the school as a mandatory mechanism of control and is assigned to authority figures, such as the superintendent, principal, and teacher. Students are assigned very little (if any) power.

. Relationships of all kinds are viewed as hierarchical power structures and well-defined roles. (Research says that authoritarian personalities often gravitate toward the ministry, the military, government, and teaching--all of which have sophisticated hierarchies of roles.)[6]

. Obedience and respect for authority are among the most important values that children must be taught.

. Punishment is the manifestation of the authoritarian's power over underlings and is a necessary tool for sanctioning behavior and teaching respect for authority.

. Because power is vested in the office or authority figure and behavior is rule-governed, student "misbehavior" is assumed to be a power play and thus a threat to the social order itself.

. Students are "given" freedom only to the extent that they consent to conform to the standards of behavior required by the sources of authority; i.e., freedom is the granted liberty to act "correctly" in accordance with the social rules, norms, and expectations of authorities in power.

When a teacher views education as an authoritarian, that teacher has a particular sensitivity to his or her own power over students. Crow and Bonney draw this unlovely portrait of such a teacher:

. . . The authoritarian often views the classroom and his position in it as a source of almost unlimited power. He may view students as objects to be manipulated, used, or bullied. . . . He probably has little patience with the concept of allowing students to voice an opinion different from his own. . . . He places an inordinately high value on order, routine, and discipline. He may, for example, have numerous minor rules which tend to become as important as course content.[7]

8

The authoritarian teacher is always asking himself (and others) such questions as "How can I make these students behave? What punishments are most effective? How can I control my class if my principal doesn't back me up?" Authoritarians are convinced that the discipline problem can best be solved by restoring the traditional authority to the role of the teacher, thus re-creating respect and obedience in students.

The authoritarian approach to classroom discipline, then, is designed to increase a teacher's power over the actions of students. Strategies usually include some combination of the following principles and practices:

(1) Rules should be clearly and firmly established by the teacher. The teacher should attempt to identify a wide variety of unacceptable behaviors and prohibit these in his or her rules for students. From a practical standpoint, rules should be short, concise, and specific. They should be **taught** to students so that there is no misunderstanding about the rule itself or about the penalties for those who break the rules.

(2) Punishments should be swiftly and consistently applied when rules are broken. Tradition has supplied a host of punishments for teachers to employ: reprimands, deprivation of privileges, isolation (in the corner or the principal's office), extra homework, and paddling--to mention but a few. Punishments serve not only as consequences to broken rules, but as reminders of the power of a teacher to create unpleasantness for students. As Dobson says, "When a youngster tries . . . stiff-necked rebellion, you had better take it out of him. Pain is a marvelous purifier."[8]

(3) As the authority figure, the teacher is the judge of misbehavior. Teachers, therefore, must have good "command presence," be ready to make quick and accurate judgments, and be alert to potential deviates. Things happen in a classroom only with the teacher's approval.

(4) A teacher's power may be enhanced by assertiveness training techniques. Frederick Jones suggests the following approach to a resisting student:

As soon as something starts, deal with it. . . . Being assertive is the key. . . . It's one thing to say "I mean business" and another thing to enforce it. . . . Put your palms flat down on his

9

desk and face him at his level. Stay there until
he caves in.[9]

Other methods from assertiveness training--such as the
"broken record" technique--are also helpful in establishing teacher authority. Here the teacher keeps
repeating his or her request (no matter what a student
says to divert the teacher) so that the student learns
that the request is serious and that the teacher will
indeed persist until compliance is achieved.

   Authoritarians, then, see power as a force vested
in roles of authority figures to be used to coerce,
command, and control the behavior of powerless students. It is manifested in directions, rules, and
demands; student failure to comply results in punishment. If punishments do not work, the teacher generally refers the problem to a **more** powerful authority--
such as the principal or eventually the board of education itself. Each level of authority in the hierarchy has more power than the one below it to employ
punishment and sanction. For example, a teacher may
send the offending student from the room; the principal may send the student home for the day; the board
may expel the student from the educational system.
Thus, power is used to enforce rules and norms in the
quest for orderly and acceptable student behavior.

   The authoritarian approach to school discipline
depends on the institutional and personal power of the
teacher. Its virtues lie in its simplicity, its long
tradition, its widespread public support, its ideal of
a harmonious social order where values of "respect"
and "efficiency" prevail. In many ways, the virtues of
the authoritarian school mirror the historical-cultural
values of a constitutional republic--where initiation
into the "power structure" of the society requires
acceptance of the rules of the social order as a pre-
requisite to full participation. Without agreed-upon
rules, roles, and standards both the republic and the
school are in danger of anarchy and lawlessness.

   On the other hand, a society which thrives on
centralized authority where power resides only at the
top of the hierarchical social structure can serve as
the prototype of a police state. It may seem ironic
that it is in a society where there is a puppet government that has no real power, where there is censorship
of the press, where attendance at "cultural assemblies"
is mandatory, and where anyone who tries to escape is
tracked down and returned to the society--in short, in

the American public schools--that we claim to be teaching **democratic** values. An excess of power in the offices of the society, and that "miniature society" (to use John Dewey's phrase) we call the school, is dangerous for democracy.

Furthermore, we know that punishment is not very effective in changing behavior. Although this staple of the authoritarian approach to discipline is well-ensconced in public school practice, its effects seem to be more negative than positive. The American Psychological Association claims that "physical violence imprinted at an early age and the modeling of violent behavior by punishing adults induces habitual violence in children."[10] At best, punishment strategies only temporarily suppress a behavior. If we know what punishment is ineffective--probably even harmful--why do educators call for even more of it? In all likelihood, a punishment survives because of its **symbolic** significance, a sharp reminder that power to inflict discomfort is the right of the authoritarian teacher.

The Behavioral Psychology Approach

A second approach to school discipline is found in the principles of behavioral psychology. Although B. F. Skinner is generally credited with the seminal research in developing this theory of "operant conditioning," earlier thinkers, dating as far back as John Locke, have contributed to the principles embraced by this approach. According to Locke, and later to Skinner and his followers, power resides not so much in authority figures as in the external environment in terms of the rewards that a person receives for certain behaviors.

In his well-known **Walden Two**, Skinner has his persona Frazier set forth the basic tenets of behaviorism:

. . . If it is in our power to create any of the situations which a person likes or to remove any situation he doesn't like, we can control his behavior. When he behaves as we want him to behave, we simply create a situation he likes or remove one he doesn't like. As a result, the probability that he will behave that way again goes up, which is what we want. Technically, it's called **positive reinforcement**. The old school made the amazing mistake of supposing the opposite was true, that by removing a situation a

11

person likes or setting up one he doesn't like--
in other words, by punishing him--it was possible
to **reduce** the possibility that he would behave in
a given way again. That simply doesn't hold. . .
.11

In his deterministic view of conditioned behavior, "the
environment takes over the rule function and role of
autonomous man . . . [and] the fact remains that it is
the environment which acts upon the perceiving person,
not the perceiving person who acts upon the environment."12

    The shared assumptions of behaviorists include
these:

- Power resides in the contingencies and consequences of behavior. To control behavior a
  teacher needs to know what rewards (reinforces)
  a student's behavior so that the reward can be
  arranged as a consequence of the desired behavior. All behavior is learned.

- Positive reinforcement is the most powerful
  shaper of human behavior. Teachers who provide
  concrete rewards (e.g., food), activity rewards
  (e.g., running errands), and social rewards
  (e.g., field trips) as payoffs for specified
  behaviors (e.g., no chatter) can increase "desired" behavior.

- Directing their behavior toward reaching specific goals in small steps of accomplishment is
  the pivotal value for children to learn. Pro-
  grammed learning operates on this principle.

- Punishment is of little educational worth, except to suppress behaviors that are clearly
  harmful to the student. Punishment may weaken
  an existing behavior but does not teach a substitute behavior.

- Because power is in the external environment,
  student misbehavior must be analyzed in terms
  of the rewards it brings the child. Scientific
  techniques of identifying and scheduling the
  rewards that modify behavior are under the control of the teacher-as-behavioral engineer.

. Students are always the end product of their conditioned responses and thus have no real freedom.

The teacher who adopts the behavioral approach frequently asks such questions as: "What will motivate this student? Am I using sufficient verbal and non-verbal praise and reinforcement? How am I unwittingly rewarding undesirable behavior?" Specific behavioral strategies include the following:

(1) Behaviors should be systematically analyzed and charted on "base lines." In many cases, students can be taught (and motivated by) the activity of charting their own behavior improvement.

(2) Rewards should be established in accordance with the needs and interests of the students whose behavior is being modified. (Actually all learning for a behaviorist is the modification of behavior.) Rewards should be paired with and immediately follow the target behavior to be strengthened (reinforced). As the behavior becomes more frequent over time, the rewards should be spaced at greater intervals on an intermittent schedule. Students can be taught to associate secondary reinforcers (praise, for example) with primary reinforcers (food, for example), eventually substituting the secondary for the primary.

(3) As the behavioral engineer, the teacher must be ever alert to environmental contingencies that shape behavior. Arranging the environment so that it produces rewards for desired behavior will control discipline problems over time.

(4) A teacher's power flows from a knowledge of the techniques of behavior modification: positive reinforcement, negative reinforcement, token economics, principles of extinction and satiation, modeling desirable behavior, and teaching cues or "prompts," for example. Teachers who apply such principles work at "catching the child being good" before giving attention or praise (positive reinforcement). If a student is disruptive, he may be sent to a "time-out" area until he can decide to behave appropriately (negative reinforcement). If a teacher has a student who throws paper at the waste can, the student can be required to stay after school to throw a few hundred more (satiation). To keep a group quietly at work, the teacher may tiptoe around the room, whispering to individuals (modeling).

Behaviorists, then, see power as a force vested in the operant conditioning process, itself always operating in the shaping of human behavior. The teacher who knows what is rewarding to given students can use that knowledge as a force to change behavior. Rewards, however, have to be skillfully arranged to be powerful reinforcers. Knowing how to pair rewards with target behaviors and how to time these rewards is crucial in effective "behavior management." Power for the teacher, consequently, is a result of the systematic and scientific techniques of training as that procedure can be "applied" to students. Finally, power for the behaviorist derives from the manipulation of consequences (pleasant and unpleasant) in terms of primary needs (e.g., food) and secondary needs (e.g., approval) of students. Thus, power to effect orderly behavior requires the teacher to employ the knowledge and techniques of the experimental psychologist in the classroom.

The behaviorist offers some alternatives to the unproductive and harmful punishment practices of the authoritarian. Managing discipline becomes a clinical, scientific process when one locates power in the external environment, the contingencies of behavior. This systematic objectification of control--through the techniques of reinforcement theory--minimizes personal power struggles between student and teacher, since the teacher's concern is not so much one of commanding respect as it is determining what consequences can be arranged that will reinforce an individual student or an entire class. To control the environment, is, indirectly, to control student behavior. The emphasis on rewards accentuates positive experiences for students, thus mitigating the negativism of punishment.

Still, there are serious social and ethical questions about behavior modification as a unilateral approach to school discipline. The Skinnerian vision of an engineered society which "shifts the determination of behavior from autonomous man to the environment"[13] suggests a totalitarian, psychologist-controlled social order potentially more authoritarian and manipulative than any police state. Abuses by teachers in the inhumane use of "aversives" (e.g., electric shocks) and "time-out" rooms (e.g., locked closets) raise doubts about educational practices growing out of behavior modification techniques. Even the reliance on extrinsic positive rewards such as candy and toys as a major control strategy is open to serious criticism.

The line between rewards and bribery is not easy to establish.

Furthermore, the implications of a depersonalized, deterministic, and mechanistic educational process where children are "shaped" toward pre-established behavioral objectives may result in a limited concept of learning and discipline. Behaviorists tend to define away such aspects of humanity as creativity, intuition, insight, freedom, and valuing because these are internal subjective states that do not lend themselves easily to objectification and scientific control. When power to determine behavior exists in the external environment, the subjective and affective dimensions are relatively insignificant to a pedagogical theory.

The Human Relations Approach

A third approach to contemporary discipline problems in schools is based on principles of humanistic education advocated by a variety of psychologists, philosophers, and educators. Many of these writers--such as Carl Rogers, Arthur Combs, William Glasser, and Thomas Gordon--are reacting against some of the values and strategies of behaviorism. This diverse group tends to see emerging school discipline problems as a consequence of poor classroom community and communication, weak self-concepts, and personal problems of students. Other shared assumptions include these:

. Power resides within individuals; therefore, the aim of education is to help each student develop personal powers and interpersonal skills to maximize human potential.

. Relationships should be personal and relatively egalitarian rather than official, hierarchical, and role-specific.

. Independence and self-worth are among the most important values that schools should develop in students.

. Punishment should be replaced by social contracts, logical consequences, conferences, and problem solving sessions.

. Because power resides in students, the teacher's role is to "facilitate" the growth and proper exercise of student power. Students are encouraged to be active participants in establishing

15

classroom rules.

. Freedom, like power, resides in the student as a
  human right. The teacher attempts to help students use their freedom constructively in accordance with democratic principles.

The humanistic educator has great faith in students
to solve their own discipline and learning difficulties. Carl Rogers characterizes this attitude when he
says:

Human beings have a natural potential for learning. They are curious about their world, they are
eager to develop and learn, and have the capacity
for making constructive discriminations between
learning opportunities. This potentiality for
learning, for discovery, can be released under
suitable conditions. . . . In short, the student's
desire to learn can be trusted. . . . Self-
initiated learning, involving the whole person of
the learner--feelings as well as intellect--is the
most pervasive and lasting.[14]

The teacher who employs the human relations
approach tends to ask such questions as: "What is
creating this problem for my students? How can I
understand the frustrations which interfere with their
healthy growth? Can the class as a whole cooperate in
the solution of our shared problems?"

Specific techniques growing out of this general
approach to school discipline include these:

(1) Rules should be mutually arrived at as part
of the social contract of the democratic classroom.
Curwin and Mendler suggest the following procedure:

We feel it is beneficial [for the teacher] to
assume the role of a group member, while maintaining control to see that the decision-making
process works effectively. However, you will
ultimately have to live by the contract and be
responsible for its implementation. . . . As a way
of avoiding mistrust we encourage you to go along
with as many rules and consequences as possible
which are agreed to by the class. . . . attempt
to reach unanimous consensus.[15]

Negotiated rules teach students how to share power
in the classroom.

(2) Logical consequences should replace punishments. Students can help determine these consequences when engaged in rule-setting. As Dreikurs explains: "There is a fine line of distinction between punishment and consequences. The child quickly recognizes the difference. Natural consequences express a logical and immediate result of the transgression, not imposed on him by an authority, but by the situation itself, by reality."[16] To send a child to the office for breaking his desk is punishment; requiring him to come back after school to help repair the desk is a logical consequence.

(3) Communication techniques should be employed to help students identify their problems and solve them. Here teachers can use Rogerian counseling--designed to **reflect** the feelings of students rather than to judge them. Gordon advocates such "communication facilitators" as passive listening, acknowledgment responses, door openers, and "active" listening.[17] The teacher is free to express his of her own feelings through "I messages," which do not attack or punish students as the cause of the teacher's angry feelings.

(4) Affective approaches should be employed to develop feelings, values, and morals. As Combs argues, "Emphathic teachers, honestly concerned with understanding how students think, feel, and perceive, are far more likely than other teachers to be liked by their students [and] have less problems with motivation and discipline. . . ."[18] Techniques such as values clarification, values analysis, and moral dilemmas can help develop the valuing and decision making capabilities of students.

Humanistic teachers, then, see power as potentiality, vested in humans who can develop in directions of autonomy, freedom, and responsibility (both personal and social). Teachers cannot use power in a coercive or manipulative fashion and expect to promote growth; they can, however, help students release (or realize) their own powers of learning, growing, deciding. Thomas Gordon describes this humanistic concept of power:

Power never influences. Coercion by a powerful teacher never educates or persuades a student. He simply chooses whether to submit, fight, or withdraw until the power pressure is off. So teachers who use power actually **lessen** their influence as transmitters of values. . . . "[U]ncontrollable"

students don't need more or better external controls. They need **internal** controls and these come
only from relationships in which their needs--as
well as those with whom they relate--are respected.[19]

Thus, power for the humanistic educator is human potential itself, which should be nurtured in students by
giving them responsibility, support, and communication
skills to promote individual self-development and human
relations in the classroom community.

The human relations model offers some alternatives
to punishment not found in the repertoire of the
authoritarian or the behaviorist. The more personal
approach to students has potential for building supportive, rather than subservient or clinical, relationships between students and between students and
teacher. Concern for communication, feelings, and
values can mitigate antagonism and power struggles in
the classroom. Respecting and nurturing the independence and active participation of students in the
contract of the miniature community are educational
activities consistent with the democratic principles
of the larger society. Surely, helping students to
learn how to make decisions (and take responsibility
for the consequences) and how to evaluate the moral
implications of decisions and behaviors can shift
responsibility for discipline to students themselves--
as maturing, responsible human beings.

On the other hand, there are many practical problems in this approach as it relates to school discipline. It takes teachers of unusual talent and personality to make the approach work. The bureaucratic,
factory-model school with large classes works against
the slow processes of personal rapport and community
solidarity. Pressures for academic/cognitive achieve-
ment--exacerbated by back-to-basics trends--de-empha-
size the affective aspects of humanistic education.
The ephemeral and passe open education movement, which
espoused similar goals in the 1960s, hardly augers
renewed emphasis on values education in the austere
1980s. Besides, humanistic education has always been
more appealing in theory than in practice. Evidence,
for example, that values clarification or moral reason-
ing programs actually reduce school discipline problems
is scant. The forces of contemporary society do not
point toward an imminent revolution to sweep humanistic
education into the public school system.

Toward a Pedagogical Approach to Discipline

My analysis of three general approaches to problems of school discipline has been intended as an assessment of the strengths and weaknesses of these approaches, and I have tried to show some parallel relationships between educational assumptions of each approach and corresponding practices advocated by proponents. Matters of pedagogy and punishment relate to the locus of power in each general model of education examined: authoritarians locate power in hierarchical offices and roles; behaviorists, in the environment surrounding the "actor"; and humanistic educators, inside the individual and within his or her classroom community.

In large measure, one's approach to school discipline will be determined by where he or she thinks (or assumes) power over human behavior resides. While such a conclusion may clarify some of the school discipline debate, it falls short of a prescription for solutions to this major--and seemingly intractable--dilemma in contemporary education. Ultimately, educators, and society itself, must create a coherent and (in my opinion) multi-faceted approach to school discipline that draws upon the best aspects of existing theory and practice.

The development of an integrated and eclectic pedagogical approach to school discipline requires educators to redefine basic assumptions about education and discipline, which might include the following new assumptions:

- Power resides in institutions and offices, in the external environment, and in individuals and communities. Teachers need to know where power over human action is in order to employ it for educational and social change.

- Educational relationships are based on roles, capacity to reinforce behavior, and personal interactions. Teachers need to understand the complex ways in which they relate to students as authority figures, managers of instruction and behavior, and human beings.

- Education is concerned with a wide variety of values, both traditional and emerging. Teachers need to know how to help students understand, evaluate, and act on personal and social values.

19

. Punishment has its proper uses in educational contexts but must be evaluated against such alternatives as positive reinforcement and social contracts. Teachers need to be able to employ disciplinary measures that are both theoretically and practically appropriate in given situations and that are consistent with a teacher's philosophy of education.

. Because power is distributed in several places (rather than focused in one), teachers need to be able to analyze the dynamics of power and its implications for instruction and discipline. Discipline is inextricably an asset of instruction.

. Students in school have freedom as humans, but there are constraints on freedom that grow out of role relationships and environmental restrictions. Teachers need to know how to use instruction and the social milieu of the classroom to teach students responsible uses of freedom. Student rights are balanced by student responsibilities; individual freedoms cannot ignore social obligations.

The specific applications of a wide variety of discipline techniques may be found in every public school: rules, token economies, time-out rooms, social contracts, behavior clinics, and problem solving sessions, for example. Most teachers probably know what their orientations to discipline are--whether toward the authoritarian end of the power continuum or toward the humanistic side. This article has been designed, in part, to help teachers clarify and expand that knowledge. Indeed, fragmented and incoherent discipline practices--varying from teacher to teacher and school to school--and poorly developed philosophies of discipline can hardly be expected to result in effective school-wide or district-wide policies and practices.

What is essential for effective practice in dealing with discipline is an integrated and fully developed philosophy of school discipline, one built on the kind of broad platform suggested here for the pedagogical model. Only when teachers and (even) total school faculties have evolved a mature and comprehensive approach--well grounded in research and theory--can we expect to see lasting solutions to the discipline problem in our public schools. Of course, we feed to have room for diversity and flexibility of management techniques within the schools; but hit-and-miss practices in handling discipline will not, in the final analysis, improve the teacher's lot. As John Dewey once noted, there is nothing so practical as a good theory. The most practical first step for teachers who want to improve school discipline is to develop a good theoretical knowledge of various approaches to this general problem. The concept of **power** is a useful one for developing such knowledge.

Education--both its ends and means--has always been characterized by diversity within a shifting, evolving, loosely-defined consensus of our society. The task before us in solving the school discipline problem is (1) to analyze the potential contributions to a workable consensus, (2) to develop a comprehensive model--what I have called "The Pedagogical Approach"--that is a workable synthesis of the more limited competing models now available[20] and (3) to implement this comprehensive model wherever possible.

Although this present discussion has only dealt with the first task area of analysis, I am confident that we can complete the final two steps in the near future. That prospect is an exciting one indeed.

NOTES

[1]In a Senate subcommittee report in 1975, Senator Birch Bayh said that violence and vandalism in the nation's schools yearly amounts to more than one-half billion dollars, 100 murders, 12,000 armed robberies, over 200,000 assaults on teachers and students, and more than 250,000 burglaries. See **Our Nation's Schools --A Report Card** (Washington, D.C.: U.S. Congress, Senate Committee on Judiciary, April 1975).

[2]The Gallup Poll, as reported in the September 1985 **Phi Delta Kappan,** indicated that for the 16th time in the last 17 years school discipline is perceived by the public as education's most important problem.

[3]See, for example, Rudolf Dreikurs et al., **Maintaining Sanity in the Classroom** (New York: Harper and Row, 1971); Charlotte Epstein, **Classroom Management and Teaching** (Reston, Va.: Reston Publishing Company, 1979); Eugene Howard, **School Discipline Desk Book** (West Nyack, N.Y.: Parker Publishing Company, 1978); Margaret Maggs, The **Classroom Survival Book: A Practical Manual for Teachers** (New York: New Viewpoints, 1980).

[4]See, for example, S. Reed, "What You Can Do to Prevent Teacher Burnout," **The National Elementary Principal**, March 1979; Andrew DuBrin et al., "Tacher Burnout: How to Cope When Your World Goes Black," **Instructor**, January 1978; B. Hendrickson, "Teacher Burnout: How to Recognize It, What to Do About It," **Learning**, January 1979; C. Ronald Brown and Patrick Carlton, "How to Conquer Stress When You Can Cope With It and When You Can't," **The National Elementary Principal**, March 1980.

[5]The following definition captures the essence of the concept: "Social power is (a) the potentiality (b) for inducing forces (c) in other persons (d) toward acting or changing in a given direction." Ronald Lippitt et al., "The Dynamics of Power," in **Group Dynamics: Research and Theory**, ed. Dorwin Cartwright and Alvin Zander (Evanston, Il.: Row & Peterson, 1960).

[6]Richard Christie and Marie Jahoda, eds., **Studies in the Scope and Method of "The Authoritarian Personality"** (Glencoe, Il.: Free Press, 1954).

[7]Mary Lynn Crow and Merle E. Bonney, "Recognizing the Authoritarian Personality Syndrome in Educators," **Phi Delta Kappan**, September 1975, p. 42.

[8]James Dobson, **Dare to Discipline** (Wheaton, Il.: Tyndale House, 1970), p. 27.

[9]Frederick Jones, "The Eye Contact Method," **Instructor**, November 1978, p. 64.

[10]As quoted by Robert J. Trotter in "This is Going to Hurt You More Than It Hurts Me," **Science News**, November 1972, p. 332. See also Roosevelt Ratliff, "Physical Punishment Must Be Abolished," **Educational Leadership**, March 1980, pp. 474-76.

[11]B. F. Skinner, **Walden Two** (Toronto: The Macmillan Company, 1948), pp. 259-60.

[12]B. F. Skinner, **Beyond Freedom and Dignity** (New York: Alfred A. Knopf Inc., 1971), pp. 176, 178-79.

[13]Ibid., p. 205.

[14]Carl Rogers, "The Facilitation of Significant Learning," in **The Psychology of Open Teaching and Learning**, ed. Melvin Silberman et al. (Boston: Little, Brown and Company, 1972), pp. 278-79.

[15]Richard Curwin and Allen Mendler, **The Discipline Book: A Complete Guide to School and Classroom Management** (Reston, Va.: Reston Publishing Company, 1980), pp. 132-33.

16Rudolf Dreikurs, **Psychology in the Classroom** (New York: Harper and Row, 1968), p. 75.

17Thomas Gordon, **TET: Teacher Effectiveness Training** (New York: Peter H. Wyden, 1974), pp. 61-64.

18Arthur W. Combs, "Humanistic Goals of Education," in **Humanistic Education Sourcebook**, ed. Donald Read and Sidney Simon (Englewood Cliffs, N.J.: Prentice-Hall, 1975), p. 97.

19Gordon, **TET**, p. 215.

20For two new texts that attempt a synthesis see Curwin and Mendler, **The Discipline Book**, and Charles Wolfgang and Carl Glickman, **Solving Discipline Problems: Alternative Strategies for Classroom Teachers** (Boston: Allyn and Bacon, 1980). See also Thomas R. McDaniel "Exploring Alternatives to Punishment," **Phi Delta Kappan**, March 1980 and "Principles of Classroom Discipline: Toward a Pragmatic Synthesis," **The Clearing House**, December 1977.

23

EXPLORING ALTERNATIVES TO PUNISHMENT:
THE KEYS TO EFFECTIVE DISCIPLINE

Beginning teachers, and experienced teachers too, are acutely aware of the importance--and the difficulty --of maintaining good classroom discipline. The public, by declaring school discipline as the number one problem in American education in 16 of 17 Gallup polls to date, joins professional educators in the recognition of this major perplexity. Indeed, the most recent Gallup analysis (as reported in the September 1985 **Kappan**) points out that "one person in four names discipline as the most important problem" and that "either the public schools have found no way to deal effectively with this problem or the public is not yet aware of measures that are being tried." No wonder Rudolf Dreikurs and Pearl Cassel contend, "Presently our school system is in a dilemma regarding discipline. The controversy over punishment cannot be resolved unless we give teachers alternative effective techniques for dealing with children who misbehave and refuse to learn."[1]

Although the Supreme Court recently refused to agree that corporal punishment is a violation of the Constitution's Eighth Amendment prohibition of "cruel and unusual punishment,"[2] nearly all the extant research suggests that corporal punishment--indeed, any form of punishment--is unhelpful at best and at worst is absolutely counterproductive to good discipline. A panel of the American Psychological Association (APA) in 1972 asserted that "physical violence imprinted at an early age and the modeling of violent behavior by punishing adults induces habitual violence in children."[3] As early as 1938 B. F. Skinner found in animal experiments that punishment (or aversive stimuli) do no more than temporarily extinguish a response while creating fear and hostility in the process.

In spite of research, pronouncements by APA and the American Civil Liberties Union (ACLU), and heavy liability to teachers who harm students through corporal punishment,[4] punishment continues to be the staple of disciplinary procedures in all too many schools. Corporal punishment has ben banned in Poland since 1783, in the Netherlands since 1850, in France since 1887, in Finland since 1890, and in Sweden since 1958. Most Communist countries, including the Soviet Union, do not allow corporal punishment in public schools.[5] And yet in the U.S. 40 states authorize corporal punishment in schools while only Massachusetts and New Jersey disallow the practice by state law. Why does punishment continue to be used daily in American public schools? Tradition, increased school crime and violence, and the failure of school systems and teacher education programs to promote effective alternatives are the probable reasons. But there **are** alternatives.

Educational theory and research--drawing from various schools of thought, philosophies, and psychological perspectives--have provided teachers with a multitude of principles and practices that are superior to punishment in establishing good school and classroom discipline. These approaches require skill and perseverance but have the potential for creating positive relationships, cooperation, and self-discipline in students. While no more than a brief description is possible here, I encourage teachers to investigate these alternatives and incorporate into their disciplinary practices the approaches that seem most compatible with their teaching styles and personal philosophies.

The Behavioral Model

Techniques of behavior modification have grown out of operant conditioning experiments over the past few decades. The behavioral approach suggests that behaviors, whether in the cognitive or the discipline area, are shaped by principles of reinforcement. Both positive and negative reinforcement are more effective in developing "desirable" student behavior than is punishment. To use this approach the teacher should:

(1) Catch the child being good and reward him. Many behavior problems result from a child's need for attention and his realization that teachers generally ignore behaving students in order to give attention to troublemakers. The squeaking wheel gets the grease. Reversing the process--by ignoring minor misbehavior to focus attention on cooperative children--is a lesson a class soon learns. The hardest part of this technique for the teacher is to be consistent, systematic, and doggedly patient. Rewards should immediately follow the behavior to be reinforced.

(2) Establish rewards that children will work for and connect these directly to "desirable" behavior. Teachers can use questionnaires, classroom discussions, and observation of what children do in their free time (a technique called "premacking") to discover those things and activities children find rewarding.

26

These rewards may then be paired with target behavior to strengthen motivation to behave appropriately. Food, toys, free time, trips, comic books, conversation breaks, special jobs, names--these are only a few of the reinforcers that an imaginative teacher can use as rewards.[6] For bigger rewards, use chips or markers as tokens that may, after accumulation to a specified number, be redeemed--as grocers use stamps of low monetary value to strengthen our tendency to shop at their places of business.

(3) Praise desirable behavior in the classroom, using positive verbal and nonverbal responses. Research tells us that teachers do not use praise effectively and, in fact, use it far less than they **think** they do. One large survey in a public school system in Florida, for example, found that 77% of the teachers' interactions with children were negative in tone.[7] Teachers need to expand their verbal praise list beyond the conventional "good," "yes," "right," and "O.K." responses. They should work at such nonverbal reinforcers as smiles, nods, touch, attention, closeness, gestures, and eye contact. Instead of writing on the board the names of misbehaving students who are to "stay in" at recess, write names of the **best**-behaved students. With a noisy class, put a check mark in a column on the board after every five minutes of quiet and give the whole class five minutes of free time if they earn, say, five checks during the period.

(4) Use "modeling" to teach appropriate behavior. Since children imitate behavior, particularly that of significant others such as peer leaders and teachers, teachers can exemplify the behavior they expect from students. When teachers try to talk over an undercurrent of classroom chatter, noisily walk around the room during a quiet-time seatwork assignment, come to class late and unorganized, and respond to "called-out" questions and comments, they are modeling the very behavior they most despair of in students. Teachers should not only model the kind of behavior they expect from students but should use well-behaved, prestigious peers as group leaders or in paired seating arrangements in order to enhance their modeling value in the classroom.

(5) Teach the cues that signal the approach of an expected behavior. Cueing can be one of the most effective techniques for eliminating situations that frequently result in punishment for children. While many teachers have developed--probably intuitively--a repertoire of cues, most teachers could benefit from a con-

scious, systematic, overt recognition that cues can be employed to create good behavior. A teacher may ring a small bell when it is time to change centers, turn the light switch on and off when it is time to put away laboratory equipment, stand before the class with a raised hand when attention is required, point to the lunch monitor when it is time to exit for lunch. But a creative teacher can go far beyond these obvious examples. In a restless and talkative class the students can be taught to cue the teacher that they know an answer by resting their heads on their desks. The teacher, of course, must then reinforce this behavior by recognizing a student who is giving the appropriate cue. Cues should be **explained** to students and **consistently** followed in the classroom.

(6) Use negative reinforcement when a child's behavior is unacceptable. Unlike punishment, negative reinforcement allows the **child** to terminate an undesirable situation when he is ready to behave. The distinction may be slight, but it is important. Sending a misbehaving child to stand in the corner for "the rest of the period" is punishment; removing him from the group to a "time out" area "until he is ready to play by the rules" is negative reinforcement. In the first case a child can only reflect upon his sins, while in the latter he can decide to change his behavior and in so doing remove the mildly undesirable condition of solitary confinement. He is more likely in this negative reinforcement situation to develop positive behaviors, whereas punishment usually generates resentment and a desire to revenge.

Because behavior modification techniques can be powerful, teachers must be sensitive to the ethical implications[8] and the practical consequences[9] of this approach.

The Human Relations Model

The human relations approach to school discipline rests on a number of psychological theories, such as those developed by Carl Rogers, Haim Ginott, Thomas Gordon, and William Purkey. Those who look at discipline from a human relations perspective propose a number of strategies that supersede punitive measures. Emphasis is generally placed on communication, democratic processes, and personal interaction in the classroom. Practical application of theory suggests that the teacher should:

28

(1) Treat students with respect and politeness. Ginott says, "A wise teacher talks to children the way he does to visitors at his home."[10] In what he calls "invitational teaching," Purkey says the focus is "on the teacher's belief system--that students are valuable, can learn, and are responsible for their conduct. The teacher communicates these beliefs within a framework of gentle but firm expectations for each student."[11]

(2) Communicate effectively by describing rather than evaluating. Ginott says, "Sarcasm is not good for children. It destroys their self-confidence and self-esteem. . . . Verbal spankings do not improve performance or personality. . . . When a child feels aggrieved, it is best to acknowledge his complaint and voice his wish. . . . 'Talk to the situation, not to the personality and character' is the cardinal principal of communication."[12] Instead of verbal punishment--what Ginott calls naming, blaming, and shaming--teachers should develop the language of acceptance, "congruent communication," and brevity of speech.

(3) Communicate effectively by reflecting feelings. This is a counseling technique developed by Rogers. Gordon outlines a hierarchy of "communication facilitators"--passive listening, acknowledgement responses, door openers, and active listening[13]--that enhances this communication skill. The essential task for the teacher-as-listener is to clarify and restate what his students are saying, giving expression to underlying feelings that seem to be causing a student's anger, fear, or frustration. When a student challenges a teacher by saying, "I'm not going to take that stupid test now," a teacher using active listening would not respond by ordering, threatening, moralizing, or punishing; instead, he would reflect what he thinks is the student's underlying feeling: "You are afraid you are not going to do well." Such a response keeps communication open, avoids "put-down" messages, and avoids the usual power struggle in confrontations.

(4) Communicate effectively by using "I-messages," a technique advocated by both Ginott and Gordon. The I-message allows a teacher to describe his own feelings--disappointment, fear, frustration--in such a way that students are not personally attacked or punished. It "avoids the negative impact that accompanies you-messages, freeing the student to be considerate and helpful, not resentful, angry, and devious."[14] These messages contain minimal negative evaluation of stu-

29

dents and do not injure personal relationships. According to Gordon, the I-message has three components: a description of the **behavior** that bothers the teacher, a statement of the tangible **effects** of that behavior, and the **feeling** that the teacher consequently has. For example: "When you have you feet in the aisle [description of behavior], I am apt to trip over them [tangible effect], and I am afraid I will fall and get hurt [feeling]."[15] This kind of communication tends to strengthen human relations and reduces the conflicts and the roadblocks to communication that so frequently end in verbal or physical punishment for students.

(5) Negotiate with students to establish rules of behavior and to find solutions to problems. William Glasser advocates the use of the classroom meeting to discuss and resolve community problems, and the "Glasser circle" is now used in many schools by teachers who are trying to involve students more responsibly in decision making. As Dennis Van Avery argues, "The process of learning responsibility can best take place between people who can really get to know each other. We need continually to be concerned about allowing small groups of young people to interact with responsible adults."[16] Gordon proposes a formal problem-solving process to deal with discipline and other shared problems in the classroom, a process that involves students in a democratic and creative way. The teacher defines the problem and facilitates a brain-storming of possible solutions (**all** are listed on the board), which are then evaluated. The class moves toward a consensus on the one solution that everyone--and that includes the teacher--is willing to try for a specified period of time.

Because the human relations approach requires an unusual range of skills and attitudes on the part of the teacher, a teacher's application of the techniques above should be developed carefully and patiently.

The Pedagogical Model

The pedagogical or preventive approach to discipline problems has grown out of research and practice. Obviously, this approach has been influenced by both behavioral research and humanistic theory--but the emphasis in the pedagogical model is on instructional practices and on specific interaction patterns involving students and teachers. There has been no shortage of advice to teachers about how to discipline; however, the focus here is on how to discipline without punishing. Among the selected principles to consider are those that argue that the teacher should:

(1) Keep discipline problems from occurring by providing structured but varied lessons. When lessons are student-centered, provide for active learning, and promote student/teacher shared planning, a good deal of the boredom and frustration that create discipline problems can be eliminated. Teachers who design purposeful multi-activity plans, and do so by incorporating high-interest materials, are applying preventive discipline.[17]

(2) Develop a repertoire of motivation techniques. Assigning projects to coincide with student interests, using "hands-on" learning experiences, making motivational statements, establishing rewards and prizes, providing for student choice wherever possible, employing instructional games, and showing personal interest in students and their educational accomplishments--all of these practices enhance student motivation. Of course, it is also important for the teacher to show involvement in and enjoyment of the class activities, thus motivating by example.

(3) Use voice control and distance management to keep the tone and pace of a class on target. A teacher should use the "soft reprimand" (rather than giving public attention to misbehaving students by using a loud reprimand), lower the voice and/or stop talking if an under-current of chatter develops (rather than trying to talk above the noise), employ pauses and voice inflection to assure voice variety. Moreover, the teacher should move **toward** individuals or small groups that are inattentive while moving **away** from students who are responding to a teacher's question. The teacher's proximity will tend to curtail inattention, while moving away from the responder will encourage him to speak louder and across a larger number of students included in the increased "stage distance."

(4) Find natural or logical consequences for student misbehavior. Dreikurs, who argues for this approach to discipline in several of his tests, defines "natural consequences" as the "natural flow of events without interference of the teacher or parent. The child who refuses to eat will go hungry. The natural consequence of not eating is hunger." He defines "logical consequences" as "arranged or applied. If the child spills his milk, he must clean it up. In this situation the consequence is tied to the act."[18] If a

31

child is late for class, asking him to make up the time at the end of the day is a logical consequence; having him copy pages from a dictionary is mere punishment. Because a child does not associate punishment with his action but with the punisher, he does not change his behavior or attitude. A natural or logical consequence teaches a student the rational reality of misbehavior. When a child is inattentive as an assignment is given, do not repeat it; when a student writes on his desk, require him to scrub the desk clean; when an instructional game gets out of hand, call it off and return to less enjoyable routine work. But in each case be sure to stress the **connection** between the behavior and the consequence.[19] Natural and logical consequences make sense to the student and help him to learn from his mistakes.

(5) Employ assertiveness training techniques when student compliance with requests is important. A teacher may occasionally need to be unusually clear and firm about a request to a misbehaving student, particularly when students are testing the limits of authority or are not convinced that a teacher means what he says. Frederick Jones describes this approach:

> Being assertive is the key. Assertiveness is 95% body language. . . . First turn and face the child. If you're not willing to commit your body in that direction, don't expect the child to respond. . . . [P]ut an edge on your voice and say the student's name in a straight, flat tone. Next, make eye contact. . . . Lean toward him. . . . Very slowly walk right up to his desk so your leg is touching it; stand and look at the child. Don't say anything, don't hurry. By that time most kids will fold.[20]

In "assertive teaching" it is particularly important to stay with your request until you know you have made your point, repeating your position or request and refusing to be diverted or ignored. This is known as the "broken record" technique. Glasser's well-known "reality therapy" theory incorporates many assertive principles, such as "be committed. . . . Don't accept excuses. . . . Never give up."[21]

There are, of course, countless other pedagogical principles that can help the effective teacher to avoid confrontations and conflicts that may result in punishment and to find ways to deal with students in non-punitive interactions.[22]

32

Because school discipline is a critical issue in education and society today, effective ways of creating healthy and happy classrooms must be an important concern of educators everywhere. It is unlikely.that much constructive learning and teaching can be found where there is violence, disruption, apathy, and conflict between students and teachers. But it is also unlikely that we can expect administrative crackdowns on misbehavior, "get-tough" attitudes by school boards, or harsh punishment by teachers to create positive learning environments within school systems. The long-term solution to the school discipline crisis is a professional staff of educators--principals, counselors, and teachers--who can work competently and humanely with students and with instruction to find alternatives to punishment.

To accomplish these ends a concentrated, cooperative effort is essential. A few specific steps could move education into an action orientation to develop and disseminate effective disciplinary practices:

. **Recommendation 1.** Educational researchers should move quickly to design and evaluate models of classroom management that integrate the most attractive aspects of existing models (such as the three described in this article). These should be meta-theoretical models that draw from theory but point toward practice.

. **Recommendation 2.** Teacher education institutions should develop courses in classroom management for preservice and inservice teachers. These should include as much observation, microteaching, and simulation as possible. Emphasis should be placed on practical strategies in the classroom.

. **Recommendation 3.** School district personnel should create projects, perhaps in conjunction with universities, that are designed to involve teachers, principals, and supervisors in ongoing classroom and schoolwide experimentation with innovative methods and techniques of management and instruction.

. **Recommendation 4.** Professional organizations should emphasize classroom management by means of conferences and publications. Preventive discipline, home/school relations, motivation through subject matter, values education and the disruptive child, educational effects of punishment, causes of school violence--all of these need even **more** attention than they have so far received from the various associations of educators.

. **Recommendation 5.** Local, state, and federal levels of government should support efforts to get at the root of the discipline problem and to develop alternatives to punishment by providing funds for pilot projects and research at the various levels. Other forms of legislation and board action--e.g., to develop comprehensive discipline codes and policies, to create support services, and to establish consultant assistance to teachers and counselors--should be explored as well.

Clearly, these are interrelated enterprises and should be coordinated for maximum benefit. Sporadic efforts in all five areas can easily be found, but increased cooperative effort is now imperative. The problems of school discipline cannot be quickly solved with Band-Aid techniques and superficial hit-and-miss methods. Because the underlying causes of our more serious discipline dilemmas, particularly in the inner cities, cut deeply into the fabric of contemporary life, solutions depend ultimately on our ability to mend that fabric. Such a task belongs to the whole society, not to teachers alone. But teachers have a central role in the process. When teachers become skilled in the humane application of alternatives to punishment--those described here and others yet to be developed[23]--they can help schools become places where students live and learn in well-regulated liberty.

NOTES

[1]Rudolf Dreikurs and Pearl Cassel, **Discipline Without Tears,** 2nd ed. (New York: Hawthorn Press, 1972), p. 11.

[2]The case, **Ingraham v. Wright** (1977), as decided on a split vote (5-4).

[3]As quoted by Robert J. Trotter in "This is Going to Hurt You More Than It Hurts Me," **Science News,** 18 November 1972, p. 332.

[4]For some of these liabilities see my "The Teacher's Ten Commandments: School Law in the Classroom," **Phi Delta Kappan,** June 1979, pp. 703-08.

[5]Tobyann Boonin, "The Benighted Status of U.S. School Corporal Punishment Practice," **Phi Delta Kappan,** January 1979, p. 395.

[6]Many recent texts in this area contain long lists of reinforcers along with explicit directions for scheduling rewards effectively. See, for example, J. Mark Ackerman, **Operant Conditioning Techniques for the Classroom Teacher** (Glenview, Il.: Scott, Foresman, 1972); John and Helen Krumboltz, **Changing Children's Behavior** (Englewood Cliffs, N. J.: Prentice-Hall, 1972); Charles and Clifford Madsen, **Teaching Discipline: Behavioral Principles Toward a Positive Approach** (Boston: Allyn and Bacon, 1970); James Walker and Thomas Shea, **Behavior Modification: A Practical Approach for Educators** (St. Louis: C. V. Mosby, 1976); Charlotte Epstein, **Classroom Management and Teaching** (Reston, Va.: Reston Publishing Company, 1979).

[7]Bertram S. Brown, "Behavior Modification: What It Is--and Isn't," **Today's Education**, January/February 1976, pp. 67, 68.

[8]See, for example, Patricia Keir, "The Teacher as Behavior Engineer," **Educational Forum**, November 1977, pp. 111-17; and James D. Long and Virginia H. Frye, **Making It 'til Friday** (Princeton, N. J.: Princeton Book Company, 1977), Chap. 8.

[9]See, for example, David L. Gast and C. Michael Nelson, "Time Out in the Classroom: Implications for Special Education," **Exceptional Children**, April 1977, pp. 461-64.

[10]Haim Ginott, **Teacher and Child** (New York: Macmillan, 1972), p. 101.

[11]William W. Purkey, **Inviting School Success: A Self-Concept Approach to Teaching and Learning** (Belmont, Calif.: Wadsworth, 1978), p. 57.

[12]Ginott, op. cit., pp. 66-84.

[13]Thomas Gordon, **TET: Teacher Effectiveness Training** (New York: Peter H. Wyden, 1974), pp. 61-64.

[14]Ibid., p. 139.

[15]Ibid., p. 144.

[16]Dennis Van Avry, "Contrasting Solutions for School Violence," **Phi Delta Kappan**, November 1975, pp. 177-178.

[17]For other suggestions in this area, see my "A Stitch in Time: Principles of Preventive Discipline," **American Secondary Education**, June 1979, pp. 52-57. Also see Stanley A. Fagan and Nicholas J. Long, "Before It Happens: Prevent Discipline Problems by Teaching Self-Control," **Instructor**, January 1976, pp. 44-47.

[18]Rudolf Dreikurs et al., **Maintaining Sanity in the Classroom** (New York: Harper and Row, 1971), p. 80. See also his **Logical Consequences: A New Approach to Discipline** (New York: Hawthorn Press, 1968) and **Discipline Without Tears** (New York: Hawthorn Press, 1972).

[19]Don Dinkmeyer and Don Dinkmeyer, Jr., "Logical Consequences: A Key to the Reduction of Disciplinary Problems," **Phi Delta Kappan**, June 1976, pp. 665- 666.

[20]Frederick Jones in "Instructor's Guide to Sanity-Saving Discipline," **Instructor**, November 1978, p. 64. See also in the same article the contribution by Lee Canter, "Be an Assertive Teacher," p. 60.

[21]William Glasser, "Ten Steps to Good Discipline," **Today's Education**, November/December 1977, p. 61.

[22]For some good practical suggestions, see Dudley Shearburn, "What to Do When You See Red!," **Teacher**, September 1977, pp. 90, 91; Marjorie L. Hipple, "Classroom Discipline Problems? Fifteen Humane Solutions," **Childhood Education**, February 1978, pp. 183-87; Dorothy Rathbun, "How to Cope in the Middle School Jungle," **Learning**, November 1977, pp. 40 ff.; Leonard Burger, "Do You Referee When You Really Want to Teach?," **Instructor**, February 1977, pp. 55-58.

[23]One new approach that has promise is transactional analysis. See Ken Earnst, **Games Students Play** (Millbrae, Calif.: Celestial Arts Publishing, 1972); Konstantinos and Constance Kravas, "Transactional Analysis for Classroom Management," **Phi Delta Kappan**, November 1974, pp. 194-97; and Joseph D. Purdy, "How to Win at Uproar," **Instructor**, August/September 1975, pp. 64-66.

CORPORAL PUNISHMENT AND TEACHER LIABILITY:
QUESTIONS TEACHERS ASK

Since we live now in an age of litigation, teachers need to be aware of their legal liabilities and to
avoid actions which might result in a court case.
Pupil punishment is an increasingly important area of
legal concern for educators. Teachers have a responsibility to protect students in their care from injury,
to act as a reasonably prudent teacher would act to
prevent loss or damage to their students, and to exercise judicious **in loco parentis** authority over students, to correct misbehavior and to provide for their
orderly instruction. Whenever a teacher is the responsible **cause** for pupil injury--which is so often the
case when punishment is involved--the possibilities of
a negligence suit are great.

But if this is an age of litigation, it is also an
age of school violence, crime, and disruption.[1] The
Supreme Court has upheld the use of corporal punishment
to discipline students (**Ingraham v. Wright**, 1977). Now
40 states authorize corporal punishment by law, with
only New Jersey and Massachusetts having laws prohibit-
ing its use.[2] With our contemporary back-to-basics
approach that stresses more law-and-order in the classroom, teachers are often expected by school boards and
administrations to exercise greater control over misbehaving students. Such an expectation is likely to
increase instances of punishment (corporal and non-
corporal) of students and, consequently, instances of
negligence cases brought against teachers. Finding
alternatives to legally dangerous punishment practices
is a high priority for educators.

The classroom teacher, caught between conflicting
forces, will need to develop greater understanding of
both the legal liabilities of improper punishment and
the effective means of establishing good discipline in
the classroom. Let us examine a few of the central
questions--legal and pedagogical--that exist or are
emerging in the area of pupil punishment and suggest
some general responses to those questions.

Questions about Pupil Punishment

. **What is corporal punishment?** This is a form of
corrective discipline that involves physical force and
the inflicting of bodily pain on the student. Typically, corporal punishment practices include paddling

37

(with or without an instrument), slapping, cracking
hands with a ruler, pinching, pushing, hitting, hammer-
locks and other wrestling holds, and exotic techniques
such as finger holds ("milk the rat") and ear twists.
In some cases, courts have extended the definition to
include threatening gestures and psychologically damaging techniques of punishment that humiliate students or
create mental anguish.

. **Does a teacher have as much authority to punish
as the parent?** No. Although the legal authority to
punish a child is granted to the teacher under the doctrine of **in loco parentis**, a teacher is not the parent
and in the eyes of the court has less authority.[3] As
student rights and the professional status of teachers
have grown in recent years, the doctrine of **in loco
parentis** has waned. Parents are liable for child
abuse, of course, but otherwise have great latitude in
punishment; teachers must justify punishment and defend
themselves against negligence charges when punishment
is arbitrary, capricious, or "excessive." Teachers may
have to prove they acted prudently and fairly in administering "moderate" punishment for corrective purposes.
Parents increasingly view teachers as highly trained
personnel in the helping professions who should be
accountable for delivering contractual services.
Courts are also expecting a higher standard of prudence
and professional expertise from teachers in negligence
cases.

. **What evidence is most damaging to a teacher
charged with excessive corporal punishment?** Probably
permanent injury to the student. Courts will not consider as "reasonable" or "moderate" punishment which dis-
figures or disables a child. In cases of mental anguish, the court may rely on expert witnesses such as
psychiatrists to establish the injury that is the basis
of this negligence suit. Although corporal punishment
is not by definition "cruel and unusual punishment,"
permanent injury may so qualify. If the injury result-
ed from aggravated attack on the student, assault and
battery charges may also be brought against the teacher.

. **In corporal punishment situation, is due process
required?** In 1975, the Supreme Court had affirmed a
lower court ruling (**Baker v. Owen**) setting up proce-
dural guidelines for corporal punishment. This decision required teachers to (1) inform students of offenses that might result in paddling; (2) punish only
in the presence of a witness; and (3) provide the

parent upon request a written explanation of the reasons. The **Ingraham** case in 1977 overturned such provision, declaring that "the Due Process Clause does not require notice and a hearing prior to the imposition of corporal punishment in the public schools. . . ." Following procedures like those outlined in **Baker** is still a good idea, however, and some states have specific requirements legislated.

. **If a teacher administers corporal punishment in anger, does a court consider that fact?** Yes, it does. Courts always consider all of the circumstances surrounding corporal punishment when a teacher is charged with negligence or assault and battery. Teachers have a professional relationship to students, are mature and prudent adults, and are to use corporal punishment only to serve an "important educational interest" (**Ingraham v. Wright**). Therefore, any evidence that a teacher has been rash or intemperate--motivated by spite, malice, or revenge--is quite detrimental to the teacher's defense. Using physical force to restrain a student from harming himself or others is justifiable unless excessive.

. **If a teacher consistently administers corporal punishment to the same degree for all offenders, does this help protect him?** No. To the contrary, common law principles suggest that it is incumbent upon a teacher to take into account the age, sex, and physical condition of each child when administering corporal punishment. That sex is to be a factor is interesting since Title IX requires **equal** treatment of boys and girls. "Physical condition" may involve size, health, and strength of the student. In short, punishment--like instruction--should be individualized.

. **What if a teacher does not know about the special health problems of a child?** This issue is less than clear in the law. The **Baker** case followed a traditional line of cases holding that if a student is supersensitive physically or emotionally to corporal punishment, the parents or the student must so declare ahead of punishment for a future case to be decided for the student on these grounds. Other precedents put greater responsibility on the educator to find out what special health problems exist. At least in some jurisdictions a teacher who, for example, strikes a hemophiliac or a child with brittle bones may be liable for resultant damages, even when the teacher is unaware of the health problem.

. **Does it matter where corporal punishment is administered on a child or with what instrument?** Yes. Since courts take all facts into consideration, they will look at both of these questions. For example, one teacher lost a suit when he struck a student on the ear, breaking an eardrum. The judge noted, "nature has provided a part of the anatomy for chastisement and tradition holds that such chastisements should be applied there."[14] Teachers have lost cases for using fists, belts, boards with holes, and other instruments deemed inappropriate for corrective punishment by the courts.

. **Can a court decide that a teacher should not have paddled a student in the first place?** Certainly. One of the issues a court considers is "substantive due process." This issue revolves around the essential question of fairness. Did the student break a rule? What was the offense? Did it merit this particular action by the teacher? Did the teacher try less severe measures first? Was the student a problem case who repeatedly failed to obey the rule in question? Since the court must decide most cases on the "reasonably prudent person" criterion, the nature of the offense is quite important in determining the reasonableness of the punishment.

. **What if parents tell teachers ahead of time not to use corporal punishment?** This is another gray area in the law. At least one court (**Glaser v. Marietta,** 1972) has ruled that a parent's wishes in this matter must be respected. The Supreme Court's **Baker** case suggested that parents should notify the school of emotional or physical health problems that could restrict the use of corporal punishment. A rule of reason is that schools should abide by a specific request from a parent not to use corporal punishment. To disregard such a request is to invite litigation.

. **Does corporal punishment work?** Well, it may relieve some of a teacher's frustration, and it does seem that some students have an almost masochistic need to be punished to satisfy a perverted "attention need." But most research says that corporal punishment at best provides a temporary cessation of the punished behavior; at worst, it creates hostility and a desire for revenge while teaching students that physical violence is a legitimate way to solve problems. The American Orthopsyhiatric Association has come out against the practice[5] as has the American Psychological Association, the latter group contending that "physical

40

violence imprinted at an early age and the modeling of
violent behavior by punishing adults induces habitual
violence in children."[6] The National Education Association and the American Civil Liberties Union[7] also
have official positions opposing corporal punishment
for legal and pedagogical reasons. Little scientific
evidence exists to support the practice.

. **Why, then, is corporal punishment so widely used
in schools today?** There are a number of possible reasons for the continuing practice: tradition, immediate
results in many cases, occasional long-term success
stories, release of anger and frustration for teachers
and administrators, expressed desire by parents and
community leaders to continue the practice, community
concern for the lack of respect for authority among
students, teachers who are untrained in discipline
techniques, and a general belief that alternatives
either do not exist or do not work. Corporal punishment is often a natural response; it is inexpensive,
quick, and relatively simple to execute.[8] Many teach-
ers--despite official position by professional groups
and a paucity of supportive evidence--honestly believe
corporal punishment to be a necessary support for the
authority of the teacher and an effective measure in
some cases.

. **What alternatives should schools and teachers be
acquainted with?** Such approaches include behavior
modification, moral education, law-related education,
suspension and in-school suspension, group counseling,
parent involvement and parent education projects,
school-within-a-school experiments, student courts and
negotiation processes, student codes of rights and
responsibilities, conflict resolution programs, after-
school behavior clinics, referral programs, "commitment" contracts, assertiveness training, transactional
analysis, humanistic curriculum modification (e.g.,
Arthur Combs's), and self-concept development strategies (e.g., William Glasser's and William Purkey's).[9]
The NEA has developed alternatives to punishment
through its Task Force on Corporal Punishment; the
National Center for the Study of Corporal Punishment
and Alternatives in the Schools is actively pursuing
research; and the National Institute of Education has
some related research projects on safe schools and
student misbehavior.

Conclusion

Pupil punishment is an increasingly important dimension of a teacher's professional life and, especially in the case of corporal punishment, an aspect of teaching that can create legal difficulties for educators. Teachers and administrators can reduce the likelihood of liability by:

- Using corporal punishment sparingly and only for a "good" reason;

- Warning students of offenses that may result in corporal punishment;

- Avoiding excessive punishment that might lead to physical or psychological injury;

- Employing moderate punishment to an appropriate part of the anatomy (**not** the head or spine) with an appropriate instrument;

- Following exactly state laws and school discipline policies governing punishment;

- Paddling only in the presence of a witness;

- Notifying parents of reasons for punishment if they request it;

- Respecting requests of parents not to use corporal punishment;

- Administering punishment in a calm manner, free of spite, malice, or revenge;

- Finding out (and communicating to student teachers and substitute teachers) any special health problems affecting punishment practices;

- Individualizing punishment to fit the nature of the offense and the age, sex, and physical condition of the child;

- Considering all consequences possible, especially if handicapped,[10] frail, or psychologically fragile children are to be punished;

- Carrying adequate liability insurance; and

. Staying abreast of legal developments in this area of school law.[11]

Given the range of punishment mishaps that could result in a negligence or assault and battery case—and given the weak pedagogical and psychological support for the effectiveness of corporal punishment—the best advice for teachers is to learn about and use a combination of alternatives to corporal punishment. These alternatives may require in-service training, extensive reading, cooperation among teachers (and support services and the community), curriculum revision, and patient dedication. For legal and educational reasons, alternatives to punishment must be pursued to keep teachers **out** of court and **in** effectively managed and well-disciplined classrooms.

NOTES

[1]The Gallup Poll, as reported in the September, 1985 **Phi Delta Kappan,** indicates that school discipline is perceived by the public to be education's greatest problem.

[2]Tobyann Boonin, "The Benightetd Status of U.S. School Corporal Punishment Practices, **Phi Delta Kappan,** January, 1979, p. 395.

[3]Richad P. Hammes, "Tort and the Teacher: Some Considerations," **The Clearing House,** October, 1979, p. 107.

[4]In the important recent case of **Hall v. Tawney** (1980), the Fourth Circuit Court of Appeals ruled on an issue of substantive due process, declaring that if corporal punishment "amounted to a brutal and inhumane abuse of official power literally shocking to the conscience," the court can assess damages against educators.

[5]For this and other cases relating to teacher torts, see my "The Teacher's Ten Commandments: School Law in the Classroom," **Phi Delta Kappan,** June, 1979, pp. 703-708.

[6]Myron Brenton, "A Further Look at Corporal Punishment," **Today's Education,** November/December, 1978, p. 53.

[7]As quoted by Robert J. Trotter in "This Is Going to Hurt You More than It Hurts Me," **Science News,** November 18, 1972, p. 332.

[8]For the ACLU's comprehensive position see Alan Reitman et al., **Corporal Punishment in the Public School** (New York: American Civil Liberties Union, 1972).

[9]Brenton, p. 54.

[10]For an examination of some of these alternatives and some bibliographical sources, see my "Exploring Alternatives to Punishment: The Keys to Effective Discipline," **Phi Delta Kappan,** March 1980. See also Eugene R. Howard, **School Discipline Desk Book** (West Nyack, New York: Parker Publishing Company, 1978); and Richard L. Curwin and Allen N. Mender, **The Discipline Book: A Complete Guide to School and Classroom Management** (Reston, Virginia: Reston Publishing Company, 1980).

[11]For an interesting treatment of this issue, see J. David Smith et al., "Corporal Punishment and Its Implications for Exceptional Children," **Exceptional Children,** January, 1979, pp. 264-268.

[12]There are several good books and articles written to advise teachers of their legal liabilities. See, for example, Daniel L. Duke et al., "Emerging Legal Issues Related to Classroom Management," **Phi Delta Kappan,** December, 1978, pp. 305-309; Chester Nolte, **How to Survive in Teaching: The Legal Dimension** (Chicago: Teach "eın, Inc., 1978); Rennard Strickland et al., **Avoiding Teacher Malpractice** (New York: Hawthorn Books, 1976); David Schimmel, Louis Fischer, and Cynthia Kelly, **Teachers and the Law** (New York: Longman, 1981).

IDENTIFYING DISCIPLINE PROBLEMS

(A Self-Evaluation Exercise)

When it comes to classroom management in the elementary school, teachers often face a variety of problems with student behavior "types." Indeed, the principles of school discipline seem to work so sporadically and unevenly because the **problems** teachers face are as variable as the students they teach; yet certain **typical** behavior problems bedevil every teacher. Below are described ten stereotypes of "problem" students almost every teacher has encountered at some time in the classroom. Which characters do you think present the most severe discipline problems? Which the least? Before reading on, put each child on what you consider to be the appropriate step of the forced-choice discipline ladder (last page of this article).

Ten Problem Children

. **Clarence** thinks he is the next Woody Allen. He seems to spend every waking moment cracking jokes, guffawing loudly and show-boating in class. If he can get a laugh at anyone's expense--including his own and that of the teacher--he will do so without hesitation. He's a regular **clown**.

. **Billy** thinks he is the Godfather. His primary purpose in life is to demonstrate how tough he is. He has learned all sorts of tough cliches, postures, and rituals. He doesn't think too much about school or the teacher--certainly not in comparison with his macho image. Billy has been known to fight at the drop of a hat and has a particular fondness for terrorizing younger children. He is a first-class **bully**.

. **Sally** must be working the third shift because she spends most of her school day sleeping. She does not bother the other kids; in fact, she is a loner. She is not only quiet and shy, she is listless and very rarely shows any interest in even your most enjoyable activities. Her quality of work is generally poor, and she rarely does homework. Sally is your **sleeper**.

. **Brenda** is always alert and cooperative. The problem is she is not very trustworthy and has a particular talent for apple-polishing. Whether or not she is genuinely interested in your lesson, she will tell you what an exciting lesson it was. She compliments your appearance at least twice a day. Always, she seems intent on manipulating you to her own advantage and to getting special favors, permissions, rewards, and attention. Brenda is a classic **brown-noser**.

. **Bradley** is immature. He sucks his thumb, cries easily and often, whines and begs like a 2-year-old. You have the feeling he will have his thumb in his mouth at age 20. He tends to hang around your desk and needs an incredible amount of assistance doing everything. He never remembers instructions. You know he is insecure, and the other kids hold him in low regard in their social order. Frequently, he grabs on to you and hovers in your footsteps. His nose is always running. Bradley is a **baby**.

. **Sarah** seems to have some latent hostility toward adults. You have the feeling she is insulting you in low whispers to her classmates while overtly smiling at you. Several times you have suspected her of devious and mischievous acts, but you can never prove it because she is wily. Whatever she can get away with--by fair means or foul--she will try. Sarah is a **sneak**.

. **Sam** is infuriating. A bright boy with a quick wit, he is unbearably sassy. He thinks he is in a personal duel with you but has judged himself the better fighter. He has no respect for authority, and his comeback remarks are cutting and impertinent. You'd really like to give him the back of your hand and wonder what his parents do with his arrogant behavior. Sam is your A-1 **smart aleck**.

. **Chad** seems totally without scruples. He seems rather average on the surface, but you have found that you have to watch him carefully. Once he took everyone's best crayons leaving his dull, short, and broken ones in return. He copies work from other kids whenever possible but always protests his innocence loudly and profusely, even in the face of overwhelming evidence. You wonder where he got his values and whether or not he will stay out of jail in later life. Chad is a **cheat**.

. **Blaze** is old beyond her years. She had her first real boy friend in kindergarten, and she has been in the social whirl ever since. You are sure that she will be a social success in later life; but her total disregard of educational matters, her nonchalance about assignments and study, her haughty maturity--so young to be so jaded--are driving you bananas. You just

46

don't seem to be able to communicate with her--maybe because she is just so blamed **blase.**

. **Harry** is perpetual motion. He is always tapping on the desk with his fingers or pencil. He slides down in his chair, twists around, swings his arms like a helicopter, and frequently falls on the floor. He is always dropping things (usually at the worst time, making the most noise) and then making a big production about picking them up. His concentration span is very short, and he can often be found wandering around the room. He creates a disturbance--maybe because he is so hyperactive. (Before reading on, place all ten children on the ladder.)

If you are like most teachers, you probably had Harry, Sam, Clarence, and Billy near the top of your ladder. These characters (frequently, but not always, boys) tend to be the most disruptive and threatening to the teacher's sense of control and order in the classroom. Dealing with these kinds of problems usually requires a teacher to have an unflappable sense of personal security, a well-structured classroom and a persistent approach to personal contact. A sense of humor is also helpful here. Each of these characters seeks attention and recognition and any boring or slow-paced lesson will provoke aggressive, high-energy behavior. The teacher who finds positive and constructive ways to meet these attention needs within the legitimate goals of the instructional program will tend to be successful with the hyperactive child, smart aleck, clown, and bully.

On the other hand, if you had students like Sarah, Bradley, and Chad at the top of your ladder, you probably have a low tolerance for dependent-passive students. Children with these kinds of behaviors (sneak, baby, cheat) usually have poor self-concepts and feelings of inferiority. Teachers may find success with these kids by providing personalized teacher encouragement, low-threat/high-success instructional strategies, and pairing with high ego strength students for activities. Praising only their acceptable behavior will also be useful in many cases.

If you had Sally, Brenda, and Blaze at the top of your ladder, you are one of a minority of teachers. These three students (frequently, but not always, girls) are least disruptive in the classroom, but are nonetheless discipline problems. Students who manifest these kinds of behaviors have found ways to cope with their inabilities and/or lack of interest in the class-

47

room in "acceptable" ways. But it is probably better
to think of students' discipline problems in terms of
the effect of their behavior on **their** learning and
social growth rather than on **your** teaching and peace of
mind. A wise teacher will be as concerned about the
sleeper and brown-noser as the bully, for each is fail-
ing to reach maximum potential in learning. Each, in
short, lacks self-discipline. These students need to
be instructionally challenged and personally counseled
in order to change their motivations and behavioral
styles. Helping such students to understand the various causes for their behavior is particularly important.

And what if your rankings violate all of the above
grouping patterns? Then you are probably acutely aware
that students in actuality come in an infinite variety
of types, and each poses a special problem for the
teacher. (Some extreme cases, of course, may require
help from counselors, psychologists, and other personnel.) In the final analysis, each student has to be
taken on his/her own terms, encouraged, nurtured,
counseled, directed, socialized, individualized, if he/
she is to develop a mature self-discipline and a healthy self-concept. Dealing with discipline is part and
parcel of the art of teaching: it comes with the terri-
tory.

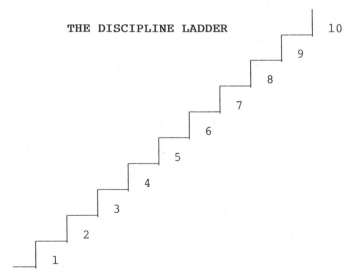

Most Severe Problem

THE DISCIPLINE LADDER

10
9
8
7
6
5
4
3
2
1

Least Severe Problem

48

PART II

STRATEGIES: Practices for the Classroom

HOW TO BE AN EFFECTIVE AUTHORITARIAN:
A BACK-TO-BASICS APPROACH TO CLASSROOM DISCIPLINE

There has been, in recent years, a plethora of models, theories, and approaches to school discipline and classroom management.[1] Teachers are urged to be humanistic or behavioristic, to use logical consequences or classroom circle discussions, to reflect feelings, use "I-messages," or negotiate behavior contracts. Furthermore, philosophers and psychologists in education keep pointing out the limitations of a negative approach to classroom conflict and the legal/educational pitfalls in corporal punishment.[2] Although all this contemporary interest in and contribution to the discipline issue in public schools is desirable--and certainly useful--the basic problem of the teacher's orientation and experience in an authoritarian system has been grossly underestimated and misunderstood by those who would ameliorate classroom conflict.

Whether one can successfully implement various approaches to classroom management of behavior depends primarily on (a) the personal philosophy, values and experience of the teacher, and (b) the educational philosophy and role expectations held by the school. It is true that both (a) and (b) are subject to change and improvement, but at any point each is given in the dynamics of discipline. I believe that most schools and most teachers are authoritarian--by nature, necessity, tradition, and definition. If this assessment is valid, then it may follow that the best way to deal immediately and successfully with discipline problems is to help teachers become effective authoritarians, carrying out their assigned responsibilities for maintaining order and peace in the classroom. Perhaps at this point a definition and defense of authoritarian education is in order.

Authoritarians, unfortunately have been too often stereotyped negatively. The very term now connotes severe, unfeeling, scowling oppression. Crow and Bonney draw this unflattering caricature of such a teacher:

. . . The authoritarian often views the classroom and his position in it as a source of almost unlimited power. He may view students as objects to be manipulated, used, or bullied. . . . He probably has little patience with the concept of allowing students to voice an opinion different

from his own. . . . He places an inordinately
high value on order, routine, and discipline.[3]

But such characterizations are no more fair to authoritarians than are the extreme characterizations of open
education teachers as permissive and weak. For example,
an authoritarian can be firm with students without
being a "bully," or can value order without placing an
"inordinately high value" on this condition.

Indeed, the authoritarian teacher is merely one
who accepts the traditional role of the authority in
the classroom. He knows that society expects teachers
to be mature and responsible leaders, to pass on the
cultural heritage, to develop values of respect and
discipline in the young. The authoritarian teacher
understands that there are standards of behavior and
performance which need to be enforced if students are
to benefit from instruction. Even more surely, he
knows that an orderly society is dependent upon students who have learned the rule of law, one of the
major values of a democratic society.

It can be argued that the authoritarian teacher
is particularly sensitive to the built-in hierarchical
power structures of modern school and contemporary
society. Indeed, research suggests that authoritarian
personalities naturally gravitate toward those social
institutions—the military, government, the ministry,
and education—where superior-inferior role relationships are most evident. Public schools are structured
so that power resides in well-defined offices. Students
are responsible to teachers who are responsible to
principals who are responsible to superintendents who
are responsible to boards of education. That is the
nature of a school, and teachers by definition must
exercise the authority of their office. This is their
major responsibility as an employee of the school
system.

In fact, the public school is (to use John Dewey's
oft quoted analogy) an "embryonic community," reflecting many of the values of the larger society. Although
the American society has sometimes been concerned with
the process of democratization—Dewey's era might be
one example, the chaotic 1960's another—it is clear
that the Reagan era is returning us to those traditional values of stability, order, and respect for authority that have always undergirded the conservative
nature of our institutions, particularly schools. As
Jenny Gray reminds us:

52

. . . From the moment he signs a contract the teacher shares with the public school a tacit obligation to society. In the main we allow ourselves to be governed by duly elected persons and their representatives. This is the only way our society can function in an orderly way. It is not good, therefore, that our young people become adept at the fine art of insurrection. The teacher who allows students to victimize him in his classroom indirectly encourages them to victimize the man at the newstand, the stranger in the park, and the cop on his beat.[4]

The school is indeed a microcosm of the world outside.

Now, if in fact most schools and most teachers are authoritarian, what sorts of disciplinary procedures follow? That is to say, if we are perforce authoritarians, how can we become truly effective in our responsibility to promote good discipline? Let me suggest a few principles and their application to the classroom.

. **Principle 1:** Rules should be clear and firm. Rules are the means by which the authoritarian teacher communicates the behavioral standards he deems necessary for the welfare of the class. He should determine unacceptable behaviors and prohibit them by rules for his students. More specifically:

(a) Rules should be **specific.** Classroom rules such as "cooperate with your fellow students," "respect your teacher," or "try hard" lack specificity and may mean widely different things to different students. I once had a teacher who claimed to have only one rule to govern behavior: "Be good." We students later figured out the twenty or so specific meanings of that rule by a painful trial-and-error process. So that students do not have to define the real meaning of a rule, state it in specific, objective terms. Such rules as "raise your hand when you have a question," "stay in your seat until the teacher dismisses you," and "keep all scrap paper in your desk until the end of the period" are clear and specific, open to very few interpretations.

(b) Rules should be **positive.** Note that in the last examples above, students are told what to **do,** not what **not** to do. Rules that begin with "don't" invite resistance and often suggest undesirable behaviors. I am reminded of Carl Sandburg's ditty: "We couldn't understand why when we came home from the store the children had beans in their ears. The last thing we told them before we went to the store was **not** to put beans in their ears." Furthermore, a positive rule suggests the solution to a problem. For example, the positive rule, "keep all scrap paper in your desk until the end of the period," lets a student know what to do with the waste paper, while the negative rule, "don't throw paper," leaves him with the unwanted paper still in his hand.

(c) Rules should be **enforced**. No rule means any more than a teacher makes it mean. Indeed, students spend a good deal of time and effort seeing if what a teacher **says** has anything to do with what he **means**. Consequently, if a teacher wants a rule to be effective, he must demonstrate that the breaking of a rule always has a consequence for the student. This consequence should immediately follow the prohibited behavior and should be consistently applied after any infraction. Enforcement usually is most effective when the consequence is (a) logically connected to the offense, e.g., staying after school for coming to class late, and (b) rehabilitative rather than punitive, e.g., washing desk tops for marking up a desk. Rules that are not enforced quickly, consistently, and logically might as well not exist. In fact, it is better to eliminate rules you cannot or will not enforce, because such rules undermine your authority.

. **Principle 2:** Teachers must use action, not anger, to control behavior. Some teachers wear themselves out yelling at students, issuing empty threats, and working themselves into a state of near hysteria all to no avail. As Dobson asks, "Have you ever screamed at your child, 'This is the last time I'm going to tell you this is the last time?'"[5] More specifically:

(a) Action should be swift and firm. "Action" implies movement rather than talk; instead of raising your voice and risking a shouting match with a defiant student, it is better to walk over to the student and simply ask him to go with you into the hall for a quick conference. As La Mancusa puts it, "at times of showdowns, it is always wiser to handle the situation with quiet and determined and decisive action. . . . Psychologists would call this action 'therapeutic bouncing.'"[6]

(b) The teacher should employ the "soft reprimand" when a student's in-class behavior needs correction. Typically, teachers tend to raise their voices when reprimanding a misbehaving student. It is more effective to

54

move toward the student and in a lowered voice to give a specific, quiet, direct command "Joe, turn around right now and start to work on the assignment." For one thing, this approach personalizes a directive; for another, it does not disrupt other students; finally, it is a private communication that does not create a public issue where a student cannot back down because of peer attention.

(c) The teacher should be assertive and employ body language to communicate authority. When students are testing a teacher's authority and resolution, it is imperative that the teacher respond effectively. Frederick Jones says, "Assertiveness is 95 percent body language. . . . First turn and face the child. If you aren't willing to commit your body in that direction, don't expect the child to respond. . . . Next, make eye contact. . . . Lean toward him. . . . Very slowly walk up to his desk so your leg is touching it; stand and look at the child. Don't say anything, don't hurry. By that time most kids will fold."[7] Another assertive discipline technique is the "broken record" in which a teacher keeps repeating his request, refusing to be diverted or ignored until the request is obeyed.

. **Principle 3:** Provide structure for the classroom and the lesson. Authoritarians know that students work and learn best in well-organized, directional, and purposeful classrooms. Routines and requirements need to be clear and ordered with understood instructions and boundaries. More specifically:

(a) Class should begin with a settling task. Students should be taught routinely when they enter class to begin work on a review drill, a "focusing event" for the new lesson, or a board-work assignment. This initial assignment becomes a control mechanism to focus students on the work at hand. During this quiet-time initial task, the teacher can quietly take roll by means of a seating chart. This structure is more effective than the teacher expectation for the students to sit down (with nothing to do!) and be quiet so that the teacher can call the roll.

(b) Students should know the objectives and activities planned for the day. It makes no sense to have structure and direction in a lesson but hide them from the students. If students are told ahead of time **what** is planned and **why** it is important and **how** the objectives will be achieved, they are likely to feel secure and purposeful under your guidance. These plans can be put on the board, the overhead, or a handout. Contracts often serve this purpose well.

(c) Classroom environments should reflect the teacher's structure. Seating arrangements, for example, are under the teacher's control. If the lesson is presentational, then traditional rows may suffice. If small-group work is in store, the teacher should make sure that tables or circles are arranged and students are assigned appropriately. At times, the teacher should manipulate lighting, furniture, and time in purposeful ways to contribute to the structural demands of a lesson. Such control communicates the leadership ability of the teacher and inspires respect and confidence from students.

Once teachers are accepted by their students as leaders, as competent instructors, as firm-but-fair disciplinarians who establish clear rules and reasonable structure, then a basis for learning and for freedom within limits exists. Defiance, disruption, and "games students play" become rarities rather than every-day, escalating, eroding misadventures. Then, and only then, can teachers begin refining and humanizing their techniques of discipline. Then, and only then, can teachers begin extending to students an opportunity for shared planning, for negotiated contracts, for full participation in rule-setting and student courts. Then, and only then, can teachers begin the important and meaningful task of democratizing the classroom.

The effective authoritarian establishes his authority only so that he can eventually relinquish his power to students, who must learn to become responsible citizens of school and society.

NOTES

[1]See, for example, Richard Curwin and Allen Mendler, **The Discipline Book: A Complete Guide to School and Classroom Management** (Reston, Va.: Reston Publishing Company, 1980); Charles Wolfgang and Carl Glickman, **Solving Discipline Problems: Alternative Strategies for Classroom Teachers** (Boston: Allyn and Bacon, 1980); Thomas McDaniel, "Exploring Alternatives to Punishment," **Phi Delta Kappan** (March, 1980).

[2]For a discussion of this issue, see my "Corporal Punishment and Teacher Liability: Questions Teachers Ask," **The Clearing House** (October, 1980), pp. 10-13.

[3]Mary Lynn Crow and Merle E. Bonney, "Recognizing the Authoritarian Personality Syndrome in Educators," **Phi Delta Kappan** (September, 1975), p. 42.

[4]Jenny Gray, **The Teacher's Survival Guide**, Palo Alto, Ca.: Fearon Publishers, 1967, p. 1.

[5]James Dobson, **Dare to Discipline**, Wheaton, Il.: Tyndale House Publishers, 1970, p. 37.

[6]Katherine C. La Mancusa, **We Do Not Throw Rocks at the Teacher**, Scranton, Pa.: International Textbook Company, 1966, p. 90.

[7]Frederick Jones, "Instructor's Guide to Sanity-Saving Discipline," **Instructor** (November, 1978), p. 64.

A STITCH IN TIME: PRINCIPLES OF
PREVENTIVE DISCIPLINE

School discipline, if we can believe the Gallup Poll, has been the number one problem in American education during the last decade. Many professional articles have dealt with such underlying causes of the problem as permissiveness in today's society, the youth culture and its concomitant alienation, changing values as a result of a changing family structure, frustration among minorities, and a general decline in respect for authority in the post-Vietnam and post-Watergate era. Manifestations of the students' malaise include vandalism, physical and verbal abuse of teachers, cheating and stealing, boredom and indifference, excessive absences and tardiness--and a host of "minor" disruptions (back-talk, clowning, room-wandering, sleeping, etc.) to further complicate the already difficult task of the classroom teacher. So what's a teacher to do?

There are many texts now available to instruct a teacher on how to solve discipline problems, how to handle disruptive students, and how to cope with a degenerating classroom management system. But the key to effective discipline is to **prevent** problems from developing, festering, and exploding in the classroom. The maxim, "A stitch in time saves nine," has no better application anywhere than in the area of school discipline. Indeed, any approach to discipline--e.g., behavior modification, humanistic psychology, democratic problem-solving--will embody principles of prevention. The difficulty is that these principles are often submerged and overpowered by the **problems** that are under consideration.

Below are a few pragmatic principles of prevention for prudent pedagogues to pursue. They are drawn rather eclectically from various theories and reflect the practices of many effective teachers.

Plan high-interest, purposeful multi-activity lessons.

The purpose of this principle is to prevent the monotony and boredom that often lead to disruption. Every teacher knows that kids who aren't "turned on" by the lesson may turn against the teacher or turn to other diversions. When lessons are student-centered, provide variety, and promote active involvement for the students in assigned (and chosen!) tasks, discipline is rarely a problem. This requires a great deal of attention to the planning process. The effective planner knows how to:

- design plans to build on identified student interests and to provide for choice;
- identify the **real** reasons for activities and assignments;
- include humor and fun in class activities;
- plan several kinds of activities for each lesson;
- plan to ensure individual and small group learning;
- intermix quiet learning (like seat work) with active learning (like games);
- plan transitions between activities, specific questions for specific students, and audio-visual instruction for almost every class;
- experiment with well-planned learning centers, outside projects, and independent research;
- diversify plans to provide for the fast-finisher and the slow learner;
- evaluate and revise plans and involve students in this process. (Cooperative teacher-pupil planning is not nearly so common as it should be.)

The teacher who works hard at the planning phase of instruction--planning the students' **learning** rather than the teacher's **teaching**--will prevent many of the causes of poor discipline in the classroom.

Prepare students for your plans.

Motivation is one of the most important prerequisites for good discipline. Indeed, planning an effective lesson is only part of the teacher's task in preventing boredom and all that derives therefrom. Unless the students are excited by your plans, know your expectations, and share your enthusiasm, the best of plans will fail. To prepare students for various aspects of a lesson, a teacher should be able to:

- make the objectives of a unit, assignment, and lesson clear;
- explain and justify every assignment (and not just by saying "You'll need this next year.");
- motivate initial learning through "advanced organizers," student experiences, and inductive techniques;
- move quickly from a motivational technique into the substantive learning, principle, or concept of the lesson;
- make instructions for the completion of the task simple and clear so that there is no confusion or ambiguity about what is expected;

. stimulate curiosity and interest through objects and
  audio-visual material related to the lesson;
. ask thought-provoking questions that require the
  students to dig deeper for answers;
. make motivational statements that reflect your own
  enthusiasm ("I think you are going to find this topic
  one of the most interesting and valuable issues we
  could study");
. use charts and graphs of student progress so that
  each student can work toward specific goals;
. design home assignments that are interesting exten-
  sions and applications of what has been learned in
  class, reinforcing concepts that have been taught
  (not simply, "Do page 45 for homework.").

     When a teacher employs the personal approach to
motivation in order to prepare students for their involvement and responsibility for learning, students
are more likely to be cooperative and task-oriented.
When that occurs, you will have eliminated many potential discipline problems.

Predict your potential discipline problems.

     Obviously, if you knew how to anticipate, say, a
disruption, a confrontation, or a case of cheating, you
would be better able to prevent it from happening. And
this is precisely what effective preventive discipliners do every day. There is a paradox, however: a
teacher needs to be able to anticipate problems but
must also **expect** good behavior, self-fulfilling prophecies being what they are. Preventive discipliners
are realistic enough to know that problems and disruptions can indeed occur but are optimistic enough to
expect the best from their charges. Predicting potential discipline problems requires that teachers be able
to:

. assess motivational problems in students and assign
  seats accordingly;
. read "body language" that suggests a student may be
  having a bad day;
. plan for "trouble zones" in the day or week; before
  and after lunch, before holidays, Fridays, rainy
  days, etc.;
. avoid or limit volatile activities if a class cannot
  handle the freedom;
. create a time-out area where a disruptive student can
  cool-off;
. provide quiet times as a means of settling a class;
. use focusing and impoverishing techniques like film-

strips and soft illumination to restrict excessive stimuli;
. greet students as they come into the classroom in the morning, after lunch, or from other activities so that quick anticipatory judgments can be made;
. use verbal and non-verbal cues (and/or switch activities) at the first sign of inattention to nip that behavior in-the-bud. (It helps to know the symptoms, like finger-drumming, eye lid drooping, and window-gazing).

Most discipline problems have symptoms that a wise teacher looks for while at the same time creating the kind of climate and conditions that anticipate and correct for undesirable behavior.

Preserve your dignity and decorum as a model for students.

It is undeniable that teachers teach behavior through example. Children learn behavior and learn it primarily through imitation. Have you ever heard a teacher literally screaming, "I want you kids to get quiet right now!"? What do students **really** learn from such an approach? The teacher who acts the way he or she would have students act can prevent many common classroom disruptions. To model appropriate behavior a teacher should:

. demonstrate a calm, organized, business-like attitude;
. use the "soft reprimand" in a firm but private manner if a student is disruptive;
. talk in a low-volume voice just loud enough to be heard easily in the back of a quiet classroom;
. wait for quiet rather than talking over a rising level of chatter;
. respect the rights of students to be recognized, to express their opinions, to have their needs met;
. engage in silent reading, essay or journal writing, experiments and problem solving (why should kids value such activities if they never see the teacher doing them?);
. be polite (Haim Ginott says treat a student as though he were a guest in your house!);
. be quiet--even tip-toe--when students are quietly working on individual assignments at their desks;
. keep self-control but show students how angry feelings can be expressed through "I-messages." (Not "You delinquents are terrible" but "When you fight I

am afraid you will hurt someone and this makes me angry.");
. be honest, admit mistakes, confess ignorance, and in other ways show that teachers are real people.

There are many behaviors--attitudes towards learning, interaction among people, manners--that are caught rather than taught, are learned by osmosis, and depend on the teacher's ability to model these behaviors in the classroom. One way to prevent undesirable behavior is to teach desirable behavior as early as possible, and a positive example has strong instructional consequences.

Praise students for good behavior and for academic success.

If there is one lesson that behavioral psychology has taught teachers it is that positive reinforcement is a powerful shaper of human behavior. All students need attention but many of them find that **mis**behavior "pays off" handsomely in terms of the attention that results. Even a teacher's hostile reprimands are more rewarding than no attention at all. Whether a teacher is pointing out the mistakes in a student's work or a fault in his behavior, he is emphasizing the negative and reinforcing the very behavior he is trying to correct. To prevent problems with praise, a teacher needs to:

. "catch the child being good" and reward that behavior in some way (even if Johnny is only in his seat five minutes, choose **that** time to give him attention and praise);
. ignore minor and non-persisting infractions;
. determine what is rewarding to a class or to the individuals. (Use a questionnaire, watch what children do in their free time, ask them to bring in favorite things, etc.);
. set easy-to-reach, short-range goals for behavior and for academic achievement so that success comes easily;
. establish rewards that children will work for;
. explore various token economies for particularly difficult classes;
. keep visible records of progress and give frequent feedback so that students can see their progress;
. expand verbal reinforcers by consciously using alternatives for "good," "right," "O.K." (Be sincere but don't be stingy!);

63

. expand non-verbal reinforcers like smiles, nods, pats-on-the-back, checks for **correct** answers, special awards;
. experiment with the reward system (unexpected rewards are often best--think up some five-minute "We've been working so well, why don't we treat ourselves to ___" rewards that you can spring on the class).

A consistent effort to define the behavior you want in your classroom followed by a systematic approach based on positive reinforcement not only sets a positive tone and clear goals for behavior, it teaches students that appropriate behavior is rewarded. It takes work and patience for a teacher to implement such an approach, but the reinforcement principle can be a powerful preventer of discipline problems.

Not even a paragon of pedagogical purity can expect to employ all of these principles of preventive discipline every day and all the time. These are not intended as cookbook recipes; indeed, the application of these principles has been left primarily to the imagination and judgment of the teacher. It is not so much the specific techniques that are at issue here as one's professional attitude. Teachers who want to improve their instruction, the climate in the classroom, and the behavior of their students will succeed if they view the task as one of preventing discipline problems through a well-planned and executed positive approach. Is an ounce of prevention worth a pound of cure? When it comes to classroom discipline, you bet it is!

PRACTICING POSITIVE REINFORCEMENT:
TEN BEHAVIOR MANAGEMENT TECHNIQUES

Almost all teachers know something about behavior modification. Somewhere in their training they have learned the importance of positive reinforcement. That "praise is better than punishment" in managing behavior has become such a truism that it is trite. And yet, negativism abounds in public school classrooms today. For most practicing teachers it is a long step between knowing the principles of positive reinforcement and using them consistently, frequently, and successfully.

One reason there is such a problem in the day-to-day practices of teachers is that the practices of behavioral psychology often run counter to the growing-up experiences of most educators. Like their parents, teachers tend to **assume** good behavior, to accept it as common-place, and to ignore it on the grounds that this somehow communicates our normal expectation for good behavior. "Let sleeping dogs lie," is a common principle of child rearing. A second reason for the infrequent use of behavioral principles in classrooms is that to be assertive and to communicate authority, teachers learn to intervene quickly to squelch misbehavior. Since many children will try to see if a teacher is alert to such things as rule testing, the vigilant teacher is often trained by students to apply "desist statements" which often start with negative terms: stop, don't, no, etc. A third reason that teachers do not frequently use positive reinforcement is that their teacher education courses seldom taught them how to apply such principles to improve discipline and classroom management. We teacher-educators often tell prospective teachers that they **should** be positive but neglect to give them specific training to show them **how to** apply the principles in specific cases.

Below I have listed ten practical and specific techniques that spring from behavioral psychology. Each of the ten principles I have suggested rests on the solid research base of Neo-Skinnerian educators and psychologists. Each principle contains a suggestion for how to put positive reinforcement to work for more effective classroom discipline.

I.   TEACH SPECIFIC DIRECTIONS

Few teachers realize how many of their discipline problems are a consequence of poor, vague, or unspecified directions. Especially in elementary school we make the mistake of assuming that children know how to perform all manner of instructional and behavioral assignments. It is not enough to tell students to begin work on their math assignment, to line up for lunch, to "get ready" for dismissal, etc. To maximize good behavior it is important for teachers to teach students exactly what is required. This takes some forethought and at least a little effort, but it is well-justified and well worth the time that it takes.

Example:

"Boys and girls, it is now time to begin work on our math assignment. When I give you the signal, I want you to (1) put all supplies away, (2) take out your math books and two pencils, and (3) quietly open your books to page 12 and do the first five problems on that page. I see that everyone is ready. Mary Lou, what are the three things that you are going to do when I give you the signal? Very good. All right, begin!" At this point the teacher should watch to see that every student is following the three simple steps to beginning the math work. The wise teacher will maximize good behavior by making expectations for behavior so clear, direct, and unambiguous, that every child will know precisely what is expected. Such expectations increase the likelihood that children will behave the way you want them to.

2. LOOK FOR GOOD BEHAVIOR

This is the "catch 'em being good" principle so central to positive reinforcement. The first principle above asks you to communicate specific and positive expectations; this second principle requires you to follow through by looking for those children who are in fact complying with the expectation. This is a particularly good place to use "positive repetitions." With this technique you simply repeat each of your specific directions as you see children following them. If one child seems **not** to be following the directions, use a positive repetition on the student closest to him if you possibly can. This technique is called "proximity praise."

Example:

You have just given the directions (for the assignment in #1 above) and then you say, "Freddy has put all his materials away; Claudette has her math book and two pencils; Clarence is starting quietly to work on the first five problems on page 12." The effect

66

that such positive repetitions can have is sometimes amazing. It is important that you remember to find the examples of good behavior rather than criticizing children who are not following expectations. Many children get special attention and special service by **mis**behaving so that teachers will provide them extra attention in the classroom. The message you want to give children is that your attention is always focused on those children who are doing what you expect them to do.

3. PRAISE EFFECTIVELY

There has been a good deal of research on effective praise. Verbal praise can be a powerful tool if teachers understand the requirements of effective praise. One of these requirements is that the teacher give descriptive details as in #2 above. The teacher should describe the specific thing he or she likes in the behavior of children. Too often we are too general in our praise, whether we want to reinforce instructional behavior or deportment. So a teacher should not merely say, "You are doing a good job on your drawing." Provide the specific descriptive details to give meaning to the general term "good job." Another important element of effective praise is to concentrate on the behavior rather than on the person. The phrase, "I like the way..." is one specific teacher assertion that can help the teacher focus on what children do rather than on who they are.

Example:

"Class, you are doing a good job on your drawing. I like the way that so many of you are using the entire page for your work. I also like the way that you are using contrasting colors to make your picture more interesting. I see that some of you are working hard to put details on your pictures of people. I like the way these details make the people look so real." Praise can be overdone, of course, and it needs to be sincere. I suspect that teachers could use more praise, especially to compliment students on how they came into the room quietly and promptly, how they started to work efficiently, how they took turns at the pencil sharpener, how they raised their hands to ask for permission to contribute in class, how they kept the classroom free of trash, etc. Some teachers even use what is called "anticipatory praise" to encourage children to behave in the way that the teacher would like: "We are about to go to lunch, class. I really appreciate your picking up the scrap paper around your desk before we leave for the lunch room." This praising **before** the fact can

67

be much more effective than the normal practice of com-
plaining about the messiness of the room.

4. MODEL GOOD BEHAVIOR

Most teachers realize that a student's behavior is
learned more from the examples provided to the students
than from the admonitions that we teachers often deli-
ver. Because students "do as we do" rather than "do as
we say," it is important that we provide appropriate
models for students to emulate. Of course, one of the
most important models for students is the teacher. One
way the teacher can model the behavior he or she wants
in the classroom is to take pains to demonstrate how
things ought to be done. Such explicit modeling is
found frequently in art rooms, gymnasiums, and auto-
motive shops. It ought to be found more frequently in
all academic classrooms. Instructionally, teachers
might model their thinking process as they approach a
math problem or a literary question by simply talking
out loud to demonstrate the teacher's learning process.
In the area of classroom management, a teacher can do
explicit modeling by demonstrating how to move from
center to center, how to enter and exit the room, how
to do such simple things as sit in chairs and raise
hands for permission to move. A quick review of the
three previous principles might suggest that, in fact,
what good behavior modifiers do is to set up situations
that allow the teacher to use **students** as models.

Example:
Consider your own behavior. Are you prompt and
well-organized when you come to class? Do you keep
your voice level, low and calm? When children are working quietly at their seats, do you tiptoe around and
whisper very softly to individuals to show that you
respect their need for quiet? You should be the best
example of the behavior you expect from your students!
Also consider your use of student models. Do you train
demonstration groups that can be used to demonstrate
how a small group discussion should be conducted? Do
you select competent students to role play good manners
in a classroom? Do you take opportunities to role play
conflict resolutions so that the students themselves
can demonstrate effective ways to solve inter-personal
problems? If not, consider ways by which you might be
more effective in using the modeling principle.

5. USE NON-VERBAL REINFORCEMENT

In a way, modeling provides good opportunities for non-verbal reinforcement. When children can **see** behaviors you expect, they learn not from words but from visual images. But you can go beyond modeling to use a variety of practices that show approval for the kind of behavior you want in a classroom. Facial expressions are especially meaningful for non-verbal reinforcement. Most teachers learn, eventually, to use smiles, nods, and touch to show approval. Truly effective behavior modifiers use a great deal of non-verbal reinforcement as they are teaching the lesson verbally. As they teach, they look at children and smile as if to say, "I see you are paying attention." Assertive discipline has made the "marble jar" an exceedingly popular non-verbal reinforcer. This is a **group** reward system.

Example:
"Class, I have this empty jar. Whenever I see you behaving well, I will drop a marble in the jar. At first I may tell you exactly why I am doing that, or on certain days I may tell you that I will only drop a marble in when I see examples of a particular behavior --such as concentration on your work, efficiency in completing assignments, or following the hand-raising rule." This kind of approach allows you to teach children to respond to your non-verbal reinforcement system. This requires that you pair verbal and non-verbal reinforcement initially, but over time you gradually phase out the verbal part of the process.

6. ESTABLISH TOKEN ECONOMIES

Principle #5 above is a simple kind of token economy. Students can quickly learn that each marble in the jar is a token that may represent, say, free time. Each token might be worth 15 seconds of free time to be cashed in at the end of the day. Or the teacher might indicate that each marble counts toward a record-playing session (music of the students' choice) to be cashed in when the students have earned, say, 100 marbles. If your classes are small, token economies can be highly individualized. Special education teachers frequently are able to establish complex and sophisticated token economies with each child rewarded on his individual reinforcement card. That is more difficult to do in regular classrooms, but sometimes can be effectively arranged with those few students who seem to need the extra structure and the extra incentive that a token economy can provide. The underlying behavioral principle here is contingency management: rewards or reinforcers are contingent upon the students' demonstrating a specified behavior. In simpler language, this is sometimes called "Grandma's rule." You may remember that Grandma's rule was that if you eat your spinach, then you could have your peach cobbler. Token economies are simply ways by which students can see their progress toward some longer range goal that is contingent upon the accumulation of successive approximations toward the goal. Tokens mark the small steps--and reward them.

Example:
    "Students, if you get every answer correct on this quiz, you will not have any homework tonight (Grandma's rule). "Boys and girls, I am keeping a record of those of you who have handed in every homework assignment during the week. Those of you who have a perfect record at the end of the week will get a special certificate to take home to your parents. Students who get four certificates will get a special field trip." (token economy).

7. PREMACK

    In the principle above, the teacher tries to determine a reward that will be reinforcing to given students. Premacking (a technique named after David Premack, who first described this idea in detail) asks the teacher to let the children determine the reinforcers for appropriate behavior. In behavioral psychology, the important qualification for a reinforcer is that the **student** wants the reward. We often use grades, for example, as reinforcers for good academic behavior on the grounds that students **want** good grades. Now, that is still true for many students, of course, but not for all students. Premacking reminds us that a reinforcer is in the eye of the beholder. To put this principle to work requires you to see things from the student's perspective, to give students an opportunity to identify those things they want for rewards, and to let the students exercise as much choice as possible in setting up any token economy.

Example:
    You might use free time as an opportunity to observe what students prefer to do when given the opportunity to exercise choice. Keep a record of those children who use their free time to (a) converse with other students, (b) do their homework, (c) sleep or rest, (d) play games, (e) read comic books. If you can

generalize about the class or identify several appropriate reinforcers that individuals seem motivated by, use your knowledge to set up a reward system that the whole class or particular individuals will embrace enthusiastically.

8. TEACH KIDS TO REINFORCE ONE ANOTHER

While an effective teacher knows how to use himself or herself to reinforce students and knows how to identify the rewards (verbal, non-verbal, token) that can be used for reinforcing expected behavior, effective teachers also know how to teach students to praise one another. Actually, if you have been following the principles outlined so far, what might well be operating in a classroom is a total system of positive reinforcement. If you, the teacher, are an effective reinforcer, you are also a good model for how people might interact with one another in positive ways. The important lesson that follows from this is that you should give students an opportunity to practice what you have been modeling in the classroom. Some teachers, following the "One Minute Manager" prescription, ask students to take one minute to tell another student what they like about his or her behavior. Students can be not only negative toward their classmates but downright cruel. Providing opportunities for students to describe **good** things they see in their classmates can be a valuable practice. What you can do with one-minute praising is to train students to be more positive and to actually use the principles of positive reinforcement in their relationships with other students.

Example:
"Students, we have a few minutes now at the end of the day to think about our behavior. I would like you to work in pairs to tell one of your classmates what they have done today that is praise-worthy. Do not discuss character or personality--only those things which your partner has done during the day that you think deserves a compliment. This should take no more than one minute; when you finish, reverse the process and let your partner compliment you on specific things you have done today that can be complimented." This can be awkward and, certainly, unnatural; however, handled skillfully, this can be one of the most important minutes in the class day. And it helps teach children to look for good behavior in classmates.

9. TEACH KIDS TO REINFORCE THEMSELVES

This is a logical extension of #8 above. Students can benefit greatly from looking at their own behavior and complimenting themselves on desirable actions, goals accomplished, and performance. Such a practice forces students to look for what is good in their behavior--which in turn can be a wonderful way to improve self-concept. This needs to be a serious, but not somber, enterprise which could well be started by self-reflection and a written assignment. Just as we as parents and teachers often do, students tend to ignore good behavior. Setting up explicit opportunities to identify one's own good behavior can counteract that neglect.

Example:
"Children, we are at the end of another highly successful day. I would like each of you to write down on a piece of paper as many responses as you can to this phrase: 'Today I learned...' When you get home be sure to share your list with a parent. Next, write down as many responses as you can to this phrase: 'My behavior was successful today because...' Here, students, you should list as many kind things that you have done for yourself or others as you can possibly think of. Now get started."

10. VARY POSITIVE REINFORCEMENT

The nine principles above should give you some ways to use a variety of positive reinforcement techniques. Do not be limited by the suggestions above, however. There are many other specific practices that you can use to keep your reinforcement practices changing and improving. Variety is the spice of life, they say, and new techniques, new reinforcers, and new ideas can help keep your classroom sparkling.

Example:
Vary any typical practices you may have by having some surprise reinforcers. If you are using the marble jar, for example, announce that the class has won some bonus marbles because of especially good behavior at the assembly program. Or, as a surprise reinforcement, cancel a homework assignment because the students have done so well on the in-class drill. Use positive notes either to parents or to students themselves. A simple personal hand-written note to a student that says "Johnny, I certainly do appreciate how hard you have been trying to remember to bring your books to class"

may do more than all of your reprimands combined. Establish a "Rewards Committee" to come up with some suggestions for reinforcers the class would like to work for. Being on the Rewards Committee could be itself an important reward. Ask students to stop their work and to imagine themselves in their mind's eye successfully performing a given task. Athletes frequently go through a mental process of reinforcing their imagined success on the tennis court or basketball court or track. Why not give your students an opportunity to do the same? "Students, we are getting ready to go out to the buses for the field trip. I want you to see yourself in your mind's eye walking quietly down the hall in single file, getting on the bus in an orderly fashion, and conversing quietly as we move. When we get back, we will compare your mental image with your actual performance. Now, is everybody ready to go?"

These ten principles of positive reinforcement can help you practice what has been so often preached to you. If you successfully apply the principles of positive reinforcement in your day-to-day work with students, you will find that you not only develop your own skills of reinforcement, but that you can help students develop theirs as well. Positive reinforcement in practice can build self-concept, develop an attitude of success, and enhance instructional motivation for students. Practicing positive reinforcement principles takes work, but it is work that can pay rich dividends for the teacher who wants to make the classroom a better place in which to live.

SO YOU WANT GOOD CLASSROOM BEHAVIOR?
DON'T PREACH IT--TEACH IT!

When I was in the third grade our teacher told us, "I only have one rule in this classroom: Be good." Now, that sounded reasonable to most of us, I am sure, but no one really had the vaguest idea what the rule **meant.** It wasn't long, however, before little Grady Fox (he is about six feet four now) pushed Bobby Rust away from the gerbil case and our teacher exclaimed, "Grady, you know the rule and **that** isn't being good!" Soon after that, a group of girls were chattering while our teacher was trying to explain something and again she cautioned: "Girls, remember the rule." And so it went.

By Christmas we had learned what "Be good" meant and, in fact, had discovered that our teacher had not one rule, but about twenty, such as:

. Do not push other children away from the gerbil cage;
. Do not talk to your classmates while the teacher is talking;
. Do not come in from recess late;
. Do not copy from your neighbor;
. Do not break into the lunch line out of turn.

Somehow or other we eventually learned what our teacher expected in the way of behavior. We also learned that if we could not "be good," we were in for a lecture on proper behavior and possibly some punishment when we did not predict her hidden rules very successfully.

Now, my third grade teacher was really quite good as a teacher, but I am convinced that she created trouble for herself that could have been prevented. In the first place, she could have made her hidden rules clear, explicit, and specific at the outset. Since we never knew specific prohibitions in advance, our class had to go through a rather painful and inefficient trial-and-error learning experience. Our teacher spent a lot of time putting out fires and defining her standards **ex post facto.** This probably led us (and her) to some resentment and frustration and may have led us to question the fairness of retributive justice. In the second place, our attempts (mostly subconscious, I am sure) to get clarification and definition of behavioral standards no doubt encouraged us to send up trail balloons--how were we to know what we could get away with if we didn't give it a try? In the third place, our teacher was always in a position of punishing and preaching which put her into a negative and often adversary relationship with her students. Teachers today need to be able to employ positive approaches to classroom discipline, to teach rather than preach the acceptable behavior that is desired, and to begin this process with youngsters as soon as they begin their schooling.

My thesis is that discipline is not something we can simply assume or demand, it is not automatic, but it can and should be taught in the kindergarten and elementary school. There is no point in lamenting the failure of all too many parents to instill "good" behavior and high standards of conduct in their offspring, nor is it useful to complain that "I was hired to teach, not be a policeman." The kids are there in your classroom and the better able you are to teach kids the skills of deportment, the happier you all will be.

Of course, if you have well-planned, well-motivated, multi-activity lessons; if you have sufficient structure, variety, and pacing; if you establish cordial and positive personal relationships with students **within** an efficient and business-like framework; if you use verbal and non-verbal reinforcement and a variety of rewards; and if you work hard to improve your classroom climate and control--you will have the elements of an effective discipline system. But in addition to these general principles of discipline, teachers need to teach the skills of behavior in much the same way that other skills are taught to children. Below is a series of steps to take in teaching a given behavior.

. **First, determine the specific behaviors that you plan to teach.** Be specific and descriptive rather than general and moralistic. Do not choose "be good" or even "don't cheat" since they are very broad and open to many definitions. Think, rather, in such terms as "test-taking behavior." Write down the behavior for yourself and (in most cases) for the benefit of your students. This step will provide specificity and descriptive clarity to ensure good communication among all members of the class and the teacher.

. **Second, discuss the behavior with your class in an objective and instructional format.** There should be no attempt to be judgmental, authoritarian, or threatening: Not "if you don't, I'll..." but "we need to learn how to...take a test."

. **Third, model the behavior you expect.** Children
can be taught much more effectively by example than by
abstract verbal generalizations. If you will show
them, even in a simulated example, the behavior they
are to learn, your chances for success will improve.
Here you can sit down, put all the books away, pick up
the test, and quietly begin your study of the questions. Model the kind of posture, concentration, and
demeanor that you want the children to emulate.

. **Fourth, put the students through a practice session, a mock test in this case.** This role playing is
important in helping students internalize certain values and develop certain habits. At this stage you
would separate charts and provide other logistical
arrangements that promote concentration and minimize
cheating.

. **Fifth, teach the students the CUES you will use
to prompt or remind them of the behavior that is required.** For example, teach the class that if anyone
forgets to concentrate on his own work, you will call
his name quietly and point alternately to your eye and
hand as a reminder to keep his eyes on his own handi-
work. Teaching cues is a crucial element in teaching
behavior.

. **Sixth, apply the learnings above systematically
at the earliest opportunity to enhance the transfer of
learning to the real life situation in the classroom.**
Remember that young children have difficulty distin-
guishing between "cooperating" and "cheating" and that
your purpose is to **teach** them the difference. After
the real test, show your appreciation for--that is,
reinforce--the good test-taking behavior the class (or
particular children) exhibited.

I have made the steps above seem time-consuming
and overly elaborate when, in fact, they are neither.
They **do** require some practice and patience, but eventually will become second nature to both teacher and
students. The important factors are the attitude of
the teacher and the clarity of the specific behaviors
being taught. Although I have used test-taking behavior as my example, such behaviors as coming into the
classroom, working in groups, putting materials and
equipment away, and exiting from the classroom can be
taught in the same manner.

When teachers approach classroom behavior as an instructional challenge--and work to identify, model, practice, execute, and reinforce these behavioral skills--they will be teaching students important lessons of conduct for the classroom and society.

TEACHER LANGUAGE/STUDENT BEHAVIOR:
SUGGESTIONS FOR TEACHERS

Good classroom discipline is a complex phenomenon. It is the result of such factors as teacher organization of the lesson, clear rules, consistent enforcement of rules, administrative and parent support systems, positive reinforcement techniques, and a teacher's human relation skills. One factor that is especially important is the use of language to affect the behavior of students. Different theories of discipline approach the teacher's use of the spoken word in varying ways, but most recognize that what teachers **say**--and how they say it--can be crucial in establishing effective classroom discipline. Below are suggestions drawn from several models of discipline; teachers who consistently use these language patterns, responses, and principles can improve student behavior in their classrooms.

1. **"I like the way..."** Trite as it may sound, the use of positive statements to describe precisely the **good** behavior that goes on in the classroom is still a very effective way to improve discipline. Most teachers know this principle of behavioral psychology but do not **practice** it. Research indicates that teachers typically spend at least twice as much time reprimanding bad behavior as they do praising good behavior. Unfortunately, reprimands give attention (often the motivation for misbehavior in the first place) to a misbehaving student, which actually increases the bad behavior. Saying (with genuine appreciation) "I like the way... Johnny and Mary walked in the hallway; ... Freddy raised his hand; ...Mary Lou cleaned up the scrap paper around her desk"--etc., etc.--can become a positive force for communicating clearly the kinds of behavior you want, recognize, and reward. Because it is more "natural" to ignore good behavior while responding to bad behavior, teachers need to make conscious efforts to find as many good behaviors as possible for "I like the way..." commendations.

2. **"WHAT are you doing?"** William Glasser suggests that one of the most fruitless, counter-productive questions a teacher asks is **"Why** are you---?" Why are you hitting Clarence? Why don't you listen when I give directions? Why can't you behave? These "why" questions usually prolong the problem, create denials and excuses, and lead to long explanations. Glasser says that a teacher who confronts a misbehaving

student with "What are you doing?" in a clinical and non-threatening fashion can get the child to consider the reality of his behavior. A teacher should not make charges ("Why are you...?") since these create defensive reactions from students. Once a child describes **what** he is doing, or has done, the teacher should ask, "Did that help you in any way?" This requires the child to make a value judgment on his own behavior. Again, a teacher must be clinical, non-threatening, and non-judgmental. Finally, a teacher should ask, "What would be a better thing to do the **next** time?" Here, the teacher is giving the student an opportunity to select a better alternative behavior. This three-question sequence can help students become more responsible evaluators of their own behavior. They will become more conscious of their actions and more analytical about the decisions they make.

3. **"I need you to..."** All too frequently, teachers who observe misbehavior use negative interventions that focus on the misbehavior. Reprimands and "Why are you..." questions fall into this category as do desist statements like "Stop!" "Quiet!" "Quit!" "Don't!" Assertive discipline advises teachers to make their wants and needs known in direct assertions: "I need you to...work on your assignment, Sally; ...look at me now, Anthony; ...listen to these instructions, students." Such statements focus on behavior and communicate in a direct, business-like way what a teacher expects students to **do**. This statement of a behavioral expectation is future-oriented and positive rather than past-oriented and negative ("Stop!"). These "I need" and "I want" statements help a teacher direct student behavior toward an unambiguous teacher expectation without chastisement from the teacher or resentment from the student. If a student protests, gives an excuse, or attempts to divert the teacher, then the teacher can say, "You have a point, but I want you to..." or "That may be true, but I need you to..." This is called "the broken record technique" since the teacher keeps coming back to the "I want" or "I need" statement--until the student sees that the teacher cannot be diverted or ignored.

4. **"When you... I... and that makes me feel..."** This is a pattern from a classic "I-message," as defined by Thomas Gordon. The I-message comes from the humanistic model of school discipline and rests on the premise that a teacher can affect behavior by honestly describing student actions and their effects on the teacher. For example, a teacher might say, "When you

put your feet in the aisle [student behavior], I might trip over them [effect on teacher] and that makes me feel nervous [feeling]." These statements are not put-downs or reprimands; they are not assertions or even requests. The teacher is using language to communicate to students a problem they are causing the teacher. If the teacher has a good relationship with the class, there is a good possibility that the I-message will prompt a constructive reaction from the students--in the case above, for example, pulling their feet out of the aisle. Such messages help teachers communicate their concerns and feelings in an open, personal, humanistic fashion that **invites** student cooperation.

Other language principles and practices that can impact on student behavior include these:

. **Talk sparingly.** The "law of three-fifths" tells us that three-fifths of the time in any classroom someone is talking and three-fifths of the time it is the **teacher.** Teachers ought to plan organized ways by which students can talk more.

. **Talk softly.** When the teacher models a quiet level of conversation, this will establish a softer tone in the classroom.

. **Talk privately.** Once children are at work, a teacher should monitor by moving quickly and quietly to individuals. Personal assistance should be given so privately that only the child being helped should hear.

. **Talk confidently.** Children have an uncanny ability to sense whether or not teachers mean what they say. When teachers give clear directions or requests with absolute confidence, students tend to comply more quickly and agreeably.

. **Talk efficiently.** When starting class or giving instructions, efficient teachers make sure that students are listening--even if it requires requests ("I need everyone to listen to this"), reprimands ("Clarence, I want you to turn around and listen"), and waiting ("Girls in the back, I am waiting for your attention."). Teachers who do this effectively will be better able to talk sparingly, softly, privately, and confidently.

Classroom discipline is an art, but like all arts requires the practitioner to use skills, make wise decisions, and practice. Effective use of language--

especially helpful, direct, positive, non-punitive words—can improve communication, relationships between teacher and students, and classroom management. How well do **you** use language to make your classroom a good place to be?

FURTHER READINGS

Assertive Discipline. Lee Canter. Lee Canter and Associates. Los Angeles, 1976.

Making It Till Friday (Third Edition). James Long et al. Princeton Book Company. New Jersey, 1985.

Reality Therapy. William Glasser. Harper and Row. New York, 1975.

T.E.T. Thomas Gordon. David McKay Company. New York, 1976.

Teacher and Child. Haim Ginott. Macmillan. New York, 1972.

When I Say No, I Feel Guilty. M. J. Smith. The Dial Press. New York, 1975.

THE TEN COMMANDMENTS OF MOTIVATION

Motivation. Getting students to **move**: move toward instructional goals, move into academic learning, move forward in the acquisition of skills and values. What teacher has not wanted to know the secrets of effective motivation? In this article I have outlined ten commandments of motivation--principles drawn from the experience of effective teachers, the theories of psychologists and educators, and the current research on effective teaching. For each commandment, I have suggested a few practical applications for the classroom teacher. Practice these principles faithfully and watch your students show more interest, involvement, participation, and achievement.

COMMANDMENT I: Thou Shalt Build an Interesting Curriculum

The key term here, of course, is **interesting**. Students are always more motivated in school studies when those studies relate to topics, ideas, experiences, and materials that children find fascinating. When planning your curriculum for the year, month, week, or day, start with the guiding question, "What would my students enjoy doing that will also correlate to my learning objectives?" Remember, no one hired you because you were dull. Boredom is the arch enemy of motivation; a high-interest curriculum is your greatest ally. Of course, much of any teacher's curriculum is prescribed, but every teacher has a measure of freedom in what he or she will teach and how it may be taught. Use that freedom to maximize **interest**.

Strategies

1. Use written questionnaires to identify particular interests and areas of interest.

2. Use values strategies (e.g., "Twenty Things I Love to Do," "Values Auction") to identify and evaluate interests. Watch what children do in their free time as a guide to what their true interests are. Plan surprise activities and instructional games.

3. Consider how student interests can be integrated into the curriculum as starting points of lessons, examples of lesson concepts, and applications of learned skills. For example, when beginning a study of mythic heroes, ask students to list their own heroes

83

from sports, television, and contemporary affairs, or to bring to class comic books they have that depict "super heroes."

4. Individualize by providing choices, so students have more opportunity to select assignments, activities, or projects that are interesting for **them**. Contracts, learning activities packages (LAPS), and centers can help provide choices.

COMMANDMENT II: Thou Shalt Set Clear Goals

Educational research supports the reasonable idea that students will "move" toward goals when they know what the goals are. The goals should be fairly specific (behavioral objectives are effective in this respect), challenging without being too difficult, and communicated as expectations for the results of learning. When planning your curriculum, units, and daily lessons, do so with a focus not on what **you** are going to "cover," but on what the **students** should be able to do when the instruction is finished.

Strategies

1. Involve students in some of the goal setting for the class and for themselves individually. Be sure **you** are clear about your objectives for students.

2. State goals in behavioral terms, e.g., "the student will be able to identify the three symbols used in the poem" rather than "the student will understand symbolism."

3. Communicate goals and objectives to students before **every** lesson, orally or in writing, e.g., "Listen kids, by the end of class today, you will be able to use the color wheel to find complementary colors. You also ought to be able to select the best color combination for your painting. Now, let's get started."

4. Evaluate student progress or mastery in relation to the specified objectives.

COMMANDMENT III. Thou Shalt Communicate High Expectations

Although goals can be one way to help students move in purposeful directions, high expectations require teachers to communicate positive attitudes that convey confidence that students **can** learn, **can** achieve,

84

and **can** succeed. Too many students have quit trying because of a fear of failure, low self-concept, and negative expectations. Teachers can motivate students by exhibiting genuine belief that every child has positive self-worth and potential for high performance. Crucial here is the attitude a teacher can develop to turn high expectations from teachers into desirable self-fulfilling prophecies for students.

Strategies

1. Set objectives that challenge, but do not intimidate, students.

2. Speak encouraging words, e.g., "I know this is difficult, but you can do it."

3. Show respect for student effort. Comment on progress; be a "booster," e.g., "Keep trying . . . you are almost there . . . thanks for your hard work."

4. **Assume** students want to learn and focus them on future success, not past failures, e.g., "Next time will you indent your paragraphs?" instead of, "Why didn't you remember to indent your paragraphs?"

COMMANDMENT IV: Thou Shalt Employ Positive Reinforcement

Most teachers know that the behavioral principle of positive reinforcement can be used as a powerful extrinsic motivator. But few teachers actually **use** this principle as effectively as they might. It is so easy to get caught in the "criticism trap": a student misbehaves to get attention, the teacher reprimands the student, the student (having gotten his or her attention need met) quiets down, the teacher (having gotten his or her need for order met) feels satisfied with the effectiveness of the negative command. But because both student and teacher have been **positively** reinforced by a negative interaction, both are likely to **increase** their respective negative behaviors. Effective employment of positive reinforcement requires understanding, skill, and practice of the principle.

Strategies

1. List all of the specific things students do that you **want** to reinforce so that you can work consistently and systematically toward rewarding them for those behaviors. This will help you look for the

85

positive.

2. Use verbal and non-verbal reinforcers--praise, smiles, touch, attention, proximity, nods, winks, etc. --immediately after any movement toward one of your "target behaviors." This can encourage students to keep moving in the right direction and help you avoid the "criticism trap."

3. Remind students of specific academic objectives or social behaviors that you will be looking for, and then acknowledge and show appreciation for examples you see, e.g., "I am watching to see who will be able to put the dinosaur bones in the right place...Good job, Freddy! You have the leg bones joined correctly at the knees and hip joints."

4. Give **specific** praise for what you can find right and successful in students' work. Low ability youngsters with weak self-concepts are especially re-sponsive to this motivational technique, e.g., not "Clarence, you missed four out of ten spelling words-- and your penmanship is awful" but, "Clarence you got six out of ten spelling words right this time, which is an improvement; and the penmanship on the last two words is exactly what I want to see you do with all your words."

COMMANDMENT V: Thou Shalt Invite Success

Students (as are we all) are motivated by success --and success breeds success. Our job as teachers is to maximize each student's chances for succeeding in his or her academic work, social growth, and personal achievements. At issue in this commandment is a teach-er's attitude, an attitude that invites success because it says in word and deed, "I am going to teach you in ways that will encourage you to do well." Unfortun-ately, research shows that teachers tend to seat lower ability students farther away from the teacher, give them less time and fewer opportunities to respond to questions, and interrupt their performance more often. The invitation to succeed motivates when it reaches all students, and is effective when a teacher genuinely believes that all students are capable.

Strategies

1. State rules positively, e.g., "Walk in the halls" rather than, "No running in the halls." Compli-ment students' success in complying with rules.

2. Maximize "right answers" by asking open-ended and multiple-right-answer questions, e.g., "What would the United States be like today if Columbus had landed on the **west** coast of America?"

3. Maximize "right answers" by changing your questions to fit the answer, e.g., "Well, 'veins' would have been a good answer if I had asked what carries blood **to** the heart; can you now tell us what takes blood **from** the heart?"

4. Challenge students with direct invitations, e.g., "This is a tough problem. Who wants to give it a try?"

COMMANDMENT VI: Thou Shalt Teach Cooperation

Teachers know how to use competition--games, contests, rewards--to promote motivation, but can also enhance motivation by actively teaching students how to cooperate in reaching academic goals. Collaborative skills do not come naturally to students, especially when many of our instructional and evaluation approaches are based on competitive assumptions and processes. For example, when students cooperate on tests they are usually reprimanded for cheating. The emphasis in schools on competition, sorting and grading students, and picking "winners" creates many "losers" as well, and losing, or even the threat of losing, is hardly motivating. Cooperation, however, can build supportive relationships and group morale, handmaidens of motivation.

Strategies

1. Assign learning tasks to students in heterogeneous pairs, triads, and small groups. (You may want to give individual **and** group grades.)

2. Develop a "skill bank" of student experts (with every student an expert in **something**) who help other students in given areas of expertise.

3. Teach small group skills (differentiated tasks and roles, leader behavior, defining group goals, etc.) directly. Let effective groups be models for other groups.

4. Have students evaluate their own group processes and effectiveness; discuss these findings in class, e.g., "How many groups got every member to

87

participate? Did leaders listen to everyone's ideas?"

COMMANDMENT VII: ⌐ Thou Shalt Demonstrate Enthusiasm

Enthusiasm is a quality that springs from the personality of the teacher, but can be developed by any instructor. We know that demonstrating a particular behavior is often the most effective way to teach it to the young. We also know that enthusiasm is both a producer and a by-product of motivation. Motivated students are enthusiastic, and enthusiastic students are motivated. So much of school life is routine and mundane that teachers and students can slip into a business-as-usual rut. But enthusiasm in the classroom is the spice that brings new zest to learning for teachers as well as students.

Strategies

1. Plan special events that break the routine, e.g., change the furniture, reassign seating, redecorate the room, change the procedure for collecting homework, invent an unusual field trip, try a new teaching technique, etc.

2. Employ motivational statements that **sell** the value of your subject matter on activity, e.g., "I've got a great poem for you today, class. I want you to listen to the music in the rhyme and visualize the pictures it creates in your mind."

3. Speed up your physical movement in the classroom: be in a hurry to get on-task (the loss of "engaged time" at the beginning of most classes is a motivation damper). Be "on your feet, not on your seat."

4. Enjoy your work--and let your students know you enjoy it--not only by being enthusiastic yourself, but also by direct statement, e.g., "I like math because . . ." "Social studies is exciting when . . ."

COMMANDMENT VII: Thou Shalt Personalize Instruction

Motivation is increased when students see a connection between a subject under study and real people. Indeed, the teacher who is generally able to show students that a classroom is about **life**, not "subject matter," is a teacher who experiences few motivation problems. Teachers can ask about any lesson, "What should this mean to my students? How does this material relate to their personal lives?" One of the strongest intrinsic motivators for all of us is **ourselves**. When a teacher talks about his or her students **to** them, instead of talking **at** them, about the information to be covered, watch the interest and attention snap into place.

Strategies

1. Greet students at the door when they enter class. Shake hands, use a "special greeting" (and expect a personal response), ask a personal question. Such personal contacts recognize the individuality of students and welcome them to the class.

2. Use touch, one of the few behaviors that consistently correlates with high ratings of effective teachers in the perceptions of students, e.g., a pat on the back, a kindly touch on the shoulder, etc. This comes more naturally to some teachers than to others, of course, but is to some extent a skill that can be developed by practice.

3. Employ personal examples and illustrations in the lesson. Students usually like being personally involved as part of the subject matter of a lesson, e.g., "Now, Robby, you and Katy walked to school today; how many steps per minute do you think you took? How many steps per minute do you predict I would take?"

4. Acknowledge personal ownership of learning, e.g., "O.K., the first group--Eric, Lori, Sally, and Blake--concluded that Poe's 'The Raven' is about an **imaginary** bird. Does anyone want them to defend their idea?"

COMMANDMENT IX: Thou Shalt Induce Readiness to Learn

Often, we try to teach before the students are ready to learn. "Get out your spelling books and turn to page six" is hardly a request that motivates students to want to study spelling. Effective motivators plan specific instructional activities that create interest in a topic about to be taught. Variously termed as "set induction," "focusing events," "advance organizers," or "grabbers," such activities arrest attention and pique the students' curiosity so that they will want to pursue the subsequent learning activity. Inducing readiness requires planning and a little imagination, but the technique can be an important motivator because of the power of anticipation.

Strategies

1. Ask thought-provoking questions that can only be answered in the activity that follows, e.g., "Who can guess how many light bulbs Edison invented before he got one to work? Let's have some estimates. Now, let's read the story about an inventor who wouldn't give up, no matter how many times he failed. Ask yourself how long **you** would have stayed with this experiment."

2. Start with an event in the school and work backward to the lesson, e.g., "Did you hear the announcements on the speaker? What descriptive adjectives did your principal use to help you visualize the new report cards? . . . O.K., today we are going to write a paragraph of description."

3. Use cartoons, pictures, newspaper headlines, taped excerpts of television programs, records, etc., to capture attention, e.g., show and discuss a headline about the President's trip to China before a lesson on the Great Wall of China; ask students to speculate on the meaning of an editorial cartoon before you begin a lesson on tariffs; play the record of a Bob Newhart parody before reading a Twain parody.

4. Construct set induction experiences, e.g., have volunteers try to communicate an idea without talking and while blindfolded as a prelude to studying the life of Helen Keller; let all the tall people go to lunch early as a prelude to a discussion of discrimination.

COMMANDMENT X: Thou Shalt Encourage Student Responses

Although inducing readiness is an instructional technique for initiating movement into the lesson, keeping students involved and participating requires special skill, especially in questioning strategies. Students need to be encouraged to respond to questions and to interact with one another during most lessons. If you are practicing the first nine commandments of motivation, you are likely to have an attitude and an orientation to the students and to instruction that will make you an effective questioner too. But there are some specialized skills that can help you be even more motivating in your interaction with students.

Strategies

1. Ask questions to find out what students know, not what they do **not** know. Avoid questions designed to trap, trick, punish, or accuse; ask questions that allow students to demonstrate what they know, believe, or value, e.g., "Mary Lou, you had some fascinating ideas in your essay on pollution. Can you share some of those with us?"

2. Give more "wait time" after a question is asked (the average wait time is only one second!): you will get longer and more thoughtful responses. If you want to motivate students to give longer responses, probe by asking, "Can you tell me more about that?" instead of the intimidating, "Why?"

3. Ask questions to which you do not know the answer; confess your ignorance and see how well the students can teach **you**, e.g., "Gosh, I don't know what causes 'continental drift.' Who has some information or ideas about that?"

4. Suspend judgment when students respond to questions. Instead of saying "right" or "not quite so," simply move to other students and get a handful of responses before commenting (your comment could be a synthesis of the responses). After a response, poll the class instead of judging, e.g., "How many of you agree with Clarence?" Polling encourages students to **listen** to each other.

These ten commandments of motivation, in the hands of a competent and conscientious teacher, can turn a routine classroom into an exciting one, a mundane lesson into a challenging one, and apathetic students into interested ones. Most important of all, these motivational principles can help teachers themselves become more positive and more motivated to be the best teachers they can be. Increasing student motivation is an imperative for all educators and may well be the secret to more "engaged time" and higher achievement in contemporary classrooms. To motivate youngsters, a teacher has to develop those attitudes, instructional skills, and motivational techniques that both research and experience identify as useful. And these develop only with a teacher's conscientious **practice**. Be a more motivating teacher: start practicing.

DEVELOPING THE SKILLS
OF HUMANISTIC DISCIPLINE

Advice to teachers about classroom management and discipline abounds. Canter[1] tells us to be assertive; Skinner[2] insists that we catch children being good and reinforce them; Glasser[3] recommends ten steps to good discipline via reality therapy. Dreikurs[4] suggests logical consequences. One recent article even argues that teachers should be more effective authoritarians.[5] Preventive discipline,[6] developmental discipline,[7] three-dimensional discipline[8]--what's a teacher to do?

My experience in working with student teachers and veteran teachers--in workshops, graduate and under-graduate courses, inservice training, and school-wide discipline projects--has led me to certain conclusions about the discipline dilemma in public schools.

Conclusion 1: Teacher training should emphasize discipline skills. Most teachers enter the profession, and persevere in it, with little or no training in school discipline techniques. This is indeed strange when discipline problems are so frequently cited as the greatest dilemma facing public schools. Public criti-cism of schools and the debilitating effects of teacher burnout are closely linked to the problems of student behavior. Few states mention behavior management in certification regulations, except perhaps for special educators. Few colleges or universities require (or even provide) courses in classroom discipline for regu-lar classroom teachers. What is provided in psychology or methods courses tends to be either theoretical and academic (such as study of reinforcement principles), or folk wisdom (such as advice to be firm but gentle, friendly but aloof--and not to smile until Christmas). Very rarely, I regret to say, do we provide teachers with actual competency-based discipline skills. Train-ing for teachers should emphasize such skills.

Conclusion 2: Teacher education should emphasize the dynamics of misbehavior in the contemporary school. Students are increasingly difficult to manage. Why this is so is open to debate; that it is so is attest-ed to me by teachers everywhere I go. The causes of misbehavior are complex, but we can speculate on some of the contributing conditions. For example, in its present integrated and mainstreamed status, our school population is more diverse than ever before. The num-ber of students from single-parent homes is on the rise

93

now that almost every other marriage ends in divorce; the number of students with emotional problems and learning problems is increasing; and the impact of drugs, alcohol, and television on student behavior is only now getting the serious study it deserves.

Conclusion 3: Teacher preparation should emphasize the coherent relationship of discipline theories and practices.[9] The plethora of discipline models confuses and confounds the practicing teacher. A few years ago, teachers were told almost nothing about professional approaches to classroom management; today the over-supply of apparently conflicting theories and techniques can result in a different difficulty for teachers: sensory overload. Where does a teacher begin in the process of making sense out of discipline strategies? What comes first--rules or relationships? Praise or punishment? Negative reinforcement or negotiation? There is no single solution to so complex and variable a problem as school discipline.

Conclusion 4: Discipline techniques should be viewed as the tools with which the teacher-as-artist works in the classroom. The teacher is more important in good discipline than the particular approaches used in the classroom. For better or worse, teaching is still an art--an art informed by scientific studies of teaching and human behavior, but an art nonetheless. Just as no sex manual can prescribe the formula for "love," so no behavior management program can prescribe the formula for "discipline." Good classroom discipline is in part an elusive quality of community and communication that grows out of the people--students and teachers--who happen to be together in that given time and place. That a teacher has faith in certain techniques, believes in the students, and expects certain behavior is surely as important to good discipline as the techniques themselves.

These conclusions can serve as basic premises in the development of an integrated approach to classroom discipline that is skill based, coherent, and humanistic. It seems to me that teachers usually move through several developmental stages or levels of professional growth, as shown in Figure 1. While there may be some overlap, each stage includes a central complex of premises, attitudes, skills, and language competencies that a teacher must master as a sound basis for the next state. In this sense, then, classroom management and discipline are developmental dimensions of professional competence.

FIGURE 1. STAGES OF DISCIPLINE DEVELOPMENT
FOR PROFESSIONAL TEACHERS

Level 1. Instructional Stage

Premise:

Effective discipline begins with a teacher's knowledge of subject matter, curriculum, and methods of instruction and evaluation.

Attitudes:

1. Schools exist to promote learning--primarily the knowledge, skills, and values embodied in the formal curriculum.
2. Teachers are responsible for organizing and presenting knowledge, skills, and values and for facilitating learning.
3. Students can learn and behave in ways that help them become capable and responsible adults.

Skills:

1. Organizing unit and daily plans for clarity, logical learning, and student success.
2. Motivating students by a variety of techniques: advance organizers, set induction, and so on.
3. Designing a range of learning experiences and teaching methods: learning centers, small- and large-group instruction, audiovisuals, games, and so on.
4. Providing evaluation and feedback in ways that provide success and monitor progress.

Language Competencies:

1. Clear written and oral expression to ensure clear communication.
2. Precise behavioral objectives.
3. Unambiguous evaluation instruments.

95

Level 2. Behavioral Management Stage

Premise:

Effective discipline requires a teacher to provide both control and support of student actions.

Attitudes:

1. Schools are repositories of cultural values of behavior and have a special responsibility to help children learn those values.
2. Teachers should work with students to develop rules for behavior and teach these rules by consistent enforcement.
3. Students should be reinforced (verbally and non-verbally) for appropriate behavior.

Skills:

1. Rule setting and teaching of rules (examples, demonstration, practice, testing).
2. Setting limits verbally and nonverbally in classroom encounters.
3. Enforcing rules by action, not anger or threats, and with logical consequences.
4. Using praise, rewards, touch, gestures, cues, and modeling to reinforce.

Language Competencies:

1. Clear, specific, assertive commands ("I need you to...") with proper gestures, eye contact, proximity, tone of voice.
2. Soft reprimand and "broken record" technique.
3. Praising ("I like the way..."), cueing, ignoring.

Level 3. Humanistic Stage

Premise:

Effective discipline depends ultimately on students developing self-discipline, internal controls for behavior, and mature decision-making processes.

Attitudes:

1. Schools exist to help students grow into responsible, wise adults.
2. Teachers need to respect the worth of students as individuals with rights, needs, and feelings.
3. Students should have opportunities to assume increasing responsibility for their own actions.

Skills:

1. Establishing participatory rule-setting and problem-solving sessions.
2. Counseling techniques.
3. Contract negotiation.
4. Making solution-oriented plans with students who break rules.

Language Competencies:

1. Stating problems clearly and brainstorming solutions.
2. Reflecting feelings, active listening, congruent communication.
3. Glasser's response-set to a rule breaker ("What are you doing? Is it helping you? What should you be doing? Can you make a plan?")

Stages of Discipline Development

First, I think teachers, especially beginning teachers, need to master the skills of classroom instruction. This includes knowing the subject matter and how to sequence it and present it; knowing how to move from concepts to objectives to methods of instruction; and knowing how to provide motivation, pacing, variety, and active involvement. Good teaching promotes good discipline. Moreover, in the absence of effective instruction, classroom management is an empty exercise, a means to no defensible end. Therefore, the basis of effective discipline is the instructional program.

Some teachers teach so well that they have relatively few behavior problems. But good instruction itself is not sufficient for today's teacher. At a second developmental level in the teacher's professional self are the skills of behavior management. At this point the teacher goes beyond instruction to deal directly with management. The objective in this stage should be to understand what is required in the way of rules, consequences, rewards, and classroom structure to ensure clarity, order, and security. How should rules be arrived at, phrased, and enforced? What rewards (reinforcers) are allowable, reasonable, and effective? Why is a teacher's use of action rather than threats essential in establishing control? At this level the assertive discipline model is particularly useful because of its focus on how to communicate teacher needs to students and how to support and reinforce acceptable student behavior.

Once teachers have mastered the pedagogical skills (level one) and the control skills (level two), they are then ready to move to level three: humanistic skills. I realize that some educators will recoil at wedding the words "humanistic" and "skills"--the latter term seems so technical. But I am convinced that such skills do exist and can be learned, just as reinforcement principles and assertiveness principles can be learned and practiced as discrete skills. The teacher-as-artist will need to integrate all such skills into a personal and professional repertoire, much as the master pianist integrates the various scales into a musical repertoire.

The humanistic approach to discipline is, perhaps, most appropriate in the secondary grades, when students have reached a higher level of maturity. But elementary students can start developing the skills of self-discipline and participatory democracy. An elementary teacher who has progressed through level three can involve children in rule setting, problem solving, and contracts. The teacher (at whatever grade level) who works at building community and communication in the classroom, treats students with respect, and expects responsible and reasoned behavior is on the road to level three. But it takes more than a humanistic attitude to achieve humanistic discipline; it takes specific skills and language competencies to implement this advanced level of discipline.

At this level, teachers need to master rather complex and sophisticated techniques of humanistic discipline. Problem-solving sessions, for example, require the teacher to serve as a mediator rather than an authoritarian. It is easier simply to decree "this is the way it has to be," but the teacher who uses humanistic discipline realizes that students who are solving problems are learning to analyze needs, brainstorm solutions to shared problems, and reach consensus on solutions with classmates and teacher. The six-step Teacher Effectiveness Training process outlined by Thomas Gordon is particularly useful here. This process requires the class to:

1. Define the problem.
2. Generate possible solutions.
3. Evaluate the solutions.
4. Decide which solution is best.
5. Determine how to implement the solution.
6. Assess how well the solution solved the problem.[10]

Teachers who have mastered humanistic discipline know that the time spent in this process pays rich dividends, not only in better discipline but in more responsible and cooperative students.

The language competence of humanistic teachers is especially important in establishing good discipline. Ginott, for example, declares that "teachers who want to improve relations with children need to unlearn their habitual language of rejection and acquire a new language of acceptance."[11] This new language addresses situations rather than personalities, describes rather than evaluates, uses "I messages" rather than "you messages," avoids commands while inviting cooperation, reflects feelings, and does not label. It is sane, congruent, and brief. "A wise teacher," says Ginott, "talks to children the way he does to visitors at his home."[12]

The reality therapy approach, while somewhat authoritarian in several respects, also depends on language competencies designed to promote students' decision-making abilities. William Glasser, who developed this approach, argues that students are rational beings who must be given opportunities to make choices, decisions, and commitments. Consequently, a teacher needs to confront students in direct and personal ways to encourage responsible self-analysis and decision making. Never, says Glasser, ask misbehaving students why they did something because that focuses on the past and on submerged motives. Ask instead, "What did you do?" in a kind, nonthreatening, nonpunitive way. This question encourages students to confront the reality of their present behavior and requires tham to analyze their decisions. Once students have verbalized what they did, Glasser recommends asking, "Did this help you or others?" This question asks students to evaluate their behavior and judge its appropriateness and worth. Finally, the teacher is asking the student to decide on an alternative behavior, a solution to a problem. This solution can become the basis for a plan, a commitment, even a contract that the teacher will help monitor in future situations.

Gordon, Ginott, and Glasser stress the importance of personal relationships, democratic communities, and helpful language; they emphasize the importance of responsible decision making and self-worth to students who are developing into autonomous adults. They--as do other humanistic educators--want to see punishment replaced by positive, solution-oriented classroom practices that involve students and teachers in counseling and negotiation processes and meaningful dialogue. All of these interactions require teachers to master a host of techniques, skills, and language patterns that are far from "natural," that indeed require a great deal of practice before the teacher becomes proficient in applying them in the classroom.

Final Thoughts

As teachers consider the problems of classroom management and discipline, they should remember that their effectiveness depends not on finding quick fixes or magic formulas. Rather, effective discipliners grow in their professional competence by developing their skills of instruction, management, and humanistic

100

problem solving. Proficiency at each stage frees a teacher to concentrate on mastering the discipline competencies of the next stage. The teacher who arrives at stage three does not leave the other two stages behind but, instead, brings his or her instructional and management competencies into balance with the human relations skills of stage three.

It is near the conclusion of stage three in the teacher's development that discipline starts to become a pedagogical art, an integration of instructional techniques, behavioral skills, and humanistic practices. Teachers at this point--as artists in discipline--are able to be not only skillful but creative and intuitive as they deal with the dynamics of classroom behavior. These are the professional conductors who orchestrate the tempo of student activities to ensure harmony; these are the weavers of the classroom tapestry who are sensitive to the tones and moods and textures of complex human interactions. Such teachers are rare, but they are beautiful to behold. Their techniques are not obvious, but the results are.

Those of us who work with teachers and attempt to help them deal with discipline problems can chart the course of teacher progress by way of the three stages outlined here--so long as we do not become enslaved by stage-theory thinking. Even a beginning teacher can start mastering some humanistic discipline techniques. What is crucial is our concept of the teacher-as-artist whose skills are but tools to be integrated into the evolving professionalism of the true educator.

NOTES

[1] Lee and Marlene Carter, **Assertive Discipline** (Sea Beach, Calif.: Canter and Associates, 1976). See also the **Assertive Discipline Follow-Up Guide** (Sea Beach, Calif.: Canter and Associates, 1981).

[2] B. F. Skinner, **The Technology of Teaching** (New York: Appleton-Century-Crofts, 1968). For a more direct application of behavioral principles to discipline, see John and Helen Krumboltz, **Changing Children's Behavior** (Englewood Cliffs, N. J.: Prentice-Hall, 1972); Charlotte Epstein, **Classroom Management and Teaching** (Reston, Va.: Reston Publishing Co., 1979); James Long and Virginia Faye, **Making It 'Til Friday** (Princeton, N.J.: Princeton Book Co., 1977).

[3]William Glasser, "10 Steps to Good Discipline," **Today's Education,** 66 (November-December 1977): 61-63. See also Glasser's **Reality Therapy: A New Approach to Psychiatry** (New York: Harper & Row, 1963) and **Schools Without Failure** (New York: Harper & Row, 1969).

[4]Rudolf Dreikurs and Pearl Cassel, **Discipline Without Tears** (New York: Hawthorn Books, 1972). See also Dreikurs and Cassel, **Maintaining Sanity in the Classroom** (New York: Harper & Row, 1971).

[5]Thomas R. McDaniel, "How to Be an Effective Authoritarian," **The Clearing House**, 55 (February 1982): 245-247.

[6]Thomas R. McDaniel, "A Stitch in Time: Principles of Preventive Discipline," **American Secondary Education,** 9 (June 1979): 52-57.

[7]Laurel N. Tanner, **Classroom Discipline for Effective Teaching and Learning** (New York: Holt, Rinehart & Winston, 1978).

[8]Richard Curwin and Allen Mendler, **The Discipline Book: A Complete Guide to School and Classroom Management** (Reston, Va.: Reston Publishing Co., 1980). See also their most recent treatment of "three-dimensional discipline" in **Taking Charge: A Practical Guide to Effective Discipline** (Reston, Va.: Reston Publishing Co., 1983).

[9]For a text that attempts to provide a coherent synthesis of discipline theory and practice, see Charles Wolfgang and Carl Glickman, **Solving Discipline Problems: Alternative Strategies for Classroom Teachers** (Boston: Allyn & Bacon, 1980).

[10]Thomas Gordon, **Teacher Effectiveness Training** (New York: Peter H. Wyden, 1974), p. 228.

[11]Haim Ginott, **Teacher and Child** (New York: Macmillan, 1972), p. 81. For an interesting discussion of the different approaches to language in the strategies of Canter, Gordon, Glasser, and Ginott, see Joan Duff Kise, "Language Usage as a Means of Maintaining Classroom Discipline," **The Clearing House**, 56 (September 1982): 12-16.

[12]**Ibid.,** p. 101.

"WELL BEGUN IS HALF DONE":
A SCHOOL-WIDE PROJECT FOR BETTER DISCIPLINE

Starting the year on the "right foot" is the key to effective classroom discipline. Obviously, of course, naturally--now tell us something **new**. Well, what's new is that a school can indeed design an in-service beginning-of-the-year project that makes a difference in attitudes and actions for teachers, students, and administrators. I want to describe an unusually successful project in school discipline at a small elementary school in Greenwood, South Carolina.

The principal of Mathews Elementary asked me to work with her and her entire staff to establish a better climate, more positive attitudes, and more effective management in a school that draws heavily from a lower socio-economic mill village population. I met with the thirty teachers (and aides) in the late spring to hear their concerns and spent a few minutes in each classroom to get a feel for problems and approaches of teachers. Problems? Student apathy, discourtesy, loudness, fighting, cheating, stealing, classroom chatter--the usual list. Approaches? Teacher-made negative rules, prohibitions, punishments, threats, and yelling--the usual list.

The principal and I decided that we would devote three full morning sessions to working with the staff just prior to the beginning of school in late August to be followed by three days of observation by me as soon as classes began. The three pre-school sessions focused on principles and practices of classroom discipline.

Session One

The first meeting dealt with an overview of theories of discipline. I presented a continuum of discipline strategies to provide a framework and used the concept of "power" to differentiate between theories. The Authoritarian Model (at one extreme) locates power in the role of the teacher and in the administrative offices of the school system. The Behavioral Model locates power in the environment and the contingencies of behavior. The Human Relations Model (at the other extreme) locates power within the student. And the Pedagogical Model locates power in the interaction between students and teacher, in the dynamics of instruction itself (see Figure 1).

FIGURE 1: A DISCIPLINE CONTINUUM

Human Relations Model			Pedagogical Model			Behavioral Model	Authoritarian Model		
Neill	Rogers	Gordon	Simon	Ernst	Dreikurs	Skinner	Canter	Glasser	Dobson
Summerhill	Client Centered Therapy	TET	Values Clarification	Transactional Analysis	Logical Consequences	Reinforcement	Assertive Discipline	Reality Therapy	Punishment

No External Control

Individual More Important Than Group or Authority

Non-Intervention Strategies

Interaction Strategies

Strict and Complete External Control

Group or Authority More Important Than Individual

Intervention Strategies

FIGURE 2

POOR RULES	GOOD RULES	BETTER RULES	PUNISHMENTS	CONSEQUENCES
1. be good	1. don't throw paper on floor	1. keep scrap paper at your desk	1. go to principal	1. clean up
2. try hard	2. don't leave assignments undone	2. complete all assignments	2. teacher lecture	2. stay in after school to finish
3. cooperate	3. don't talk while the teacher is talking	3. raise your hand when you want to talk	3. detention	3. teacher ignores contribution
4. respect one another	4. don't hit classmates	4. settle arguments by discussion	4. paddling	4. time out

RULE:

1. students will come to class on time
2. students will stay in seats unless given permission to get up
3. students will work quietly during tests

CONSEQUENCES

1. a) make up time after school
   b) detention
   c) loss of free time privileges
   d) parent conference with teacher/administrator
   e) any student who is always on time may _____

FIGURE 3

DISCIPLINE AND MANAGEMENT EVALUATION FORM

TEACHER _____ CLASS _____ DATE _____

	SUPERIOR	SATISFACTORY	NEEDS IMPROVEMENT
A. PLANNING/PREVENTION			
1. Room and materials ready			
2. Objectives made clear to students			
3. Variety of activities prepared			
4. Involvement and application planned			
5. Rules for conduct clear			
6. Structure of lesson clear			
7. Motivation provided			

COMMENT:

B. EXECUTION/ACTION			
1. Lesson begins promptly			
2. Knowledge conveyed with confidence			
3. Disruptions observed and handled quickly and firmly			
4. Expectations for behavior communicated clearly and authoritatively			
5. Verbal correction (firm but non-punitive)			
6. Non-verbal correction (gestures, proximity)			
7. Private correction (soft reprimand)			
8. Pacing of lesson			
9. Reinforcement of behavior			
10. Follow-through/ consequences for misbehavior			
11. Transitions			
12. Closing class			

COMMENT:

C. PERSONAL STYLE/RAPPORT			
1. Assertiveness/command presence			
2. Movement			
3. Energy level			
4. Modeling (courtesy/quiet)			
5. Radar			
6. With-itness			
7. Friendliness/positive attitude			
8. Sensitivity to AGMs			
9. Fairness			

COMMENT:

After examining some of the basic principles and practices that follow from each theory, we gave special attention to the Authoritarian Model, whose premise is that a teacher needs to have good rules, clear and effective consequences for infractions, and "command presence" in the classroom. It is my belief that because schools are in fact (if not theory) authoritarian institutions, teachers need first and foremost to be comfortable with their own authority in the classroom. To illustrate this approach, I showed a movie "Glasser on Discipline," which presents William Glasser outlining his effective program of rule-setting and rule-enforcing techniques. We concluded this session with a rule-setting exercise. Each grade-level group designed three classroom, two hall, and two cafeteria rules that were (1) unambiguous, (2) specific, (3) short, and (4) positive.

Session Two

The next day we went over the homework so that teachers could see the diversity of values and practices they had. We returned briefly to the issue of rules, this time to look at the relationship of rules to punishments and consequences. Teachers measured their collective rules from the day before against the prototypes in Figure 2 and then went to work refining their rules and sequencing consequences for each rule as in the sample one in Figure 2, "Students will come to class on time."

Following this phase of training, we turned our attention to the more positive dimension of reinforcement. While clear rules matched with effective consequences can establish proper parameters of authority for the teacher, it is essential that the teacher reward the behavior he or she wants to perpetuate. We discussed the principles of reinforcement (well known to most teachers) and set to work on another small-group exercise to list reinforcers that these teachers could actually use. A simple list was provided to each grade-level group.

After generating a master list of concrete, activity, and social reinforcers, we worked on verbal and non-verbal reinforcement practices through a role playing activity. Teachers paired off and took turns going through this four-step exercise:

1. One teacher assumes the role of student, the other the role of teacher.

106

2. The student raises hand to answer a question from teacher.

3. The teacher says (without looking at the student), "Can you tell me the answer?"

4. When student answers question, teacher says (without emotion), "O.K."

The scenario is repeated, but this time at step #3 the teacher looks at student, smiles, moves toward student, says "Thank you, Sally, for raising your hand--what is your answer?"

At step #4 the teacher nods and gives a specific verbal reinforcer with enthusiasm (such as, "Right on target, Sally; you figured out that addition problem very quickly!").

After both teachers had an opportunity to practice praising, several particularly skilled praisers demonstrated their ability for the rest of the staff.

We concluded this session with some additional modeling exercises, one to show the importance of the teacher using a soft voice while circulating among children doing seat-work and one to show a range of cues teachers and students can use to communicate nonverbally.

Session Three

The final session brought together the rule-enforcement dimension and the positive reinforcement dimension. We viewed another film, this one on "Assertive Discipline in the Classroom" featuring Lee Canter. Canter's emphasis on **action** by the teacher when a rule is violated--rather than hostility or threats or constant pleading--is especially valuable. His sequence of consequences (name on board as warning, check beside name fifteen minutes after school, two checks beside name call to parents, etc.) gave teachers a concrete system for enforcing rules. The teachers also were intrigued by his use of marbles and a large jar to provide positive reinforcement. He explained to his students that each time he found them working well, behaving well, demonstrating courtesy, raising hands particularly well, etc., he would drop a marble in the jar. Each marble represents fifteen seconds of free time (or whatever reward the teacher deems appropriate) which the students collect when the jar is full (or at the end of the day or week). This can be an effective whole-class token economy.

Next, teachers paired off to role play an assertive discipline technique Canter calls the "broken record." In this exercise (as in the praising exercise) there is a teacher and a student, and roles switch at the end of the first role play:

1. The student engages in disruptive behavior.

2. The teacher says (without looking at the student), "Behave yourself."

3. The teacher looks at student and says, "Behave yourself."

4. The teacher looks at student, points to him and says, "John, I want you to behave."

5. The teacher looks at student, points to him, walks toward him, puts a hand on his shoulder, leans toward him and says, "John, I want you to behave right now."

This is to be done quietly, unemotionally, and firmly. Once students learn that the teacher will indeed follow through with enforcement, testing of limits steadily decreases.

Finally, we practiced some techniques from the Human Relations Model, such as conflict negotiation, effective "I-messages," and problem solving steps (as advocated by Thomas Gordon in **Teacher Effectiveness Training**). Teachers wrote up on posters their common classroom rules, leaving room for one or two additional regulations as needed by individual teachers, and readied themselves for the first day of school.

Follow-Up Observations

During the first three full days of school, I observed in each classroom for a half-hour followed by a twenty to thirty minute conference with the teacher. I designed a special instrument that would permit specific feedback on management and discipline practices we had worked on in the pre-school sessions (see Figure 3).

Conclusion

The first week of classes at Mathews Elementary astounded us all. Teachers were confident and well organized; students were calm and respectful; the halls were incredibly quiet; and the principal was ecstatic. The exemplary mood may not last indefinitely, but (as the phrase goes), "Well begun is half done." The teachers will need to keep working on (1) praising, (2) reinforcing, (3) modeling, (4) cueing, and (5) enforcing. They will need to find new and better reinforcers and to work even harder on motivation. But they know now that their students can be taught to behave properly (and to enjoy the calmer, more controlled climate!) and, even more importantly, that as teachers they have the ability to manage and discipline students in a fair, effective, professional way.

Several factors contributed to the overall success of this inservice project. First (and perhaps most important) was the leadership of the principal. Teachers knew from the outset that she initiated the project, was willing to support them, and was going to be an active participant throughout the inservice training. Second was the design of the project. Not only was there a close connection between theory and practice, there was the opportunity for each teacher to get prepared--with rules, consequences, enforcement techniques, positive reinforcement techniques, etc.--to begin the school year with a program of preventive discipline. Establishing the proper setting events (both time and place) was a crucial element in the success of the project. Third was school-wide consensus on discipline policies and practices. As teachers worked together, they created a unified and mutually supportive approach to the school's discipline problems.

In the process the teachers, aides, and principal developed an esprit de corps and positive attitudes that gave them a new confidence and a new enthusiasm for the difficult job of educating the young. The principal plans to relieve each teacher for a while each month so that a peer observation system can be developed to perpetuate the early success of this project. And who knows where that may lead? Out of such acorns have mighty oak trees grown.

PART III

CONCLUSION: A Synthesis of Theory and Practice

A PRIMER ON CLASSROOM DISCIPLINE:
PRINCIPLES OLD AND NEW

What does a teacher have to do to establish class-room control of student behavior? Fifty years ago the topic was virtually ignored in teacher education programs. Teachers then were told to "have a good lesson plan," "be firm but gentle/friendly but aloof," and "don't smile until Christmas." Not so long ago the behaviorists developed some interesting insights into re-enforcement principles, and we were told to "catch the child being good--and ignore bad behavior." Then the humanists came along and told us that good discipline was related to self-concept and communications, reminding us (as Ginott says) that "a wise teacher talks to children the way he does to visitors at his home." Now we are told to be assertive, negotiate, analyze trans-actions--and use logical consequences, reality therapy, and TET. The contemporary teacher suffers from sensory overload when it comes to discipline techniques for the classroom.

It is not just that we have more theories now, either. Everyone--from burned out teachers to the Gallup Poll to the unending Commission reports--tells teachers that discipline has to improve if the quality of education in American schools is going to rise above mediocrity. And then, finally, there is the volume of new research on effective schools and teachers. The researches are telling us that there are specific teaching techniques that lead to better learning **and** better behavior and that we need to master these techniques if we expect to have well-managed, effective classrooms. So, what's a teacher to do?

Although all of the attention to discipline from theorists, the public, and researchers **can** be confusing, there is reason for hope for the beleaguered teacher. Discipline is a complex phenomenon, as much an art as a science, and a phenomenon that is reflected in complex relationships between the teacher, the student, the lesson, and the school environment. Yet there does appear to be an emerging set of principles that make sense as general guidelines for **teacher behavior** related to effective group management and control. Like most principles, these are no better than the teachers who make them work, but I offer the following ten principles as an eclectic combination of traditional and modern, practical and theoretical, pedagogical and psychological techniques that teachers

can make work for better discipline:

1. The Focusing Principle

This principle has a good deal of traditional support from experienced teachers. It says, in effect, get everyone's attention before giving instruction or instructions. Beginning teachers, especially, make the mistake of trying to teach over chatter and inattention. They make the mistake of thinking that if they begin the lesson (and there are **many** beginning points within each lesson), students will catch on and will subside when the teacher is a few sentences--or paragraphs--into the lesson. This may in fact work on occasion. But, unfortunately, what the students really learn is that the teacher is willing to compete with them, to forge over the undercurrent, to tolerate inattention, to condone chatter while the teacher is presenting or instructing.

The focusing principle reminds teachers that they must--in group instruction--request, demand, expect, and wait for attention before instructing. A teacher can say "I am ready to begin"; "I am ready to begin, boys in the back"; "I am ready to begin, Robert, and I am waiting for you." The teacher may need to be loud at this point, to flip the light switch, stand with hand raised, ring a bell--but he or she should insist on, work for, and secure attention **first**. Then the teacher can use a calm, low-volume voice to begin actual instruction. A good, in-charge, "on-top" beginning is not repressive authoritarianism; it is the essential first ingredient in a well-mannered classroom.

2. The Direct Instruction Principle

The key to this discipline guideline is getting students on task quickly and keeping them on it consistently. (This is easier said than done, of course.) The research on direct instruction has limits since not all learning lends itself to direct instruction in the way, say, drill work on basic skills does. Nonetheless, in most classrooms there is too much wasted time and not enough "time-on-task" or "engaged time." As far back as Jacob Kounin's classic work on group management in the 1960's, researchers confirmed the common sense notion that children who were kept on task were generally kept out of trouble. But how do you get kids on task?

114

Among the specific techniques that can help expand "time-on-task," one of the most effective is the use of explicit positive expectations stated by the teacher. Here the teacher works at clear, direct statements about the assignment, the directions, and the time for work: "Your task is here on the board, class; you need to use your text and the data bank forms to collect information; and you have only ten minutes to work, so start right now." With some classes it helps to set explicit goals: "We took five minutes yesterday just distributing the construction paper; today let's see if we can distribute the paper in **three** minutes." Keeping students on task requires teacher attention to the type of tasks (interesting, relevant, varied) and to motivation of the lesson. The next few principles also help the teacher maintain student engaged time.

3. The Monitoring Principle

Essentially, "monitoring" means keeping a constant check on student performance and behavior. It requires teachers to be alert, to make a point of making personal contact with each student during a lesson, and (especially) to circulate among the students frequently. When students know the teacher is not only interested in their good work and behavior but will also evaluate these "up close and personal," they are more likely than not to stay on task. They tend to see the teacher as one who follows through and who holds students accountable for their work and behavior.

Monitoring encourages the teacher to **move** more and to engage students in personal conferences of brief duration. This personal attention and encounter allows teachers to initiate individualized directives or provide feedback. Often the focus may be on the academic task at hand ("Freddy, your triangles look fine but remember to label your angles") or on behavior ("Mabel, put your comb away and begin your math problems, please"). In either event, the private and personal conversations--carried on in a quiet voice--can have a significant effect on classroom discipline.

4. The Modeling Principle

Long before behavioral psychologists told us students' behavior could be influenced by "models," good teachers recognized the power of setting good examples for better discipline. Teachers who are courteous tend to teach courtesy by their actions.

(As the old adage puts it, "Values are caught--not taught".) Likewise, teachers who are prompt, organized, enthusiastic, self-controlled, and patient tend to produce students who exhibit--at least to some degree--similar characteristics. It takes sensitivity and tact, but teachers can also employ students as models to be emulated by their peers.

One especially important modeling technique that helps classroom discipline is a teacher's practiced use of a soft, low-volume voice. This works especially well in combination with the focusing and monitoring principles. A loud, high-pitched voice generates kinetic energy in a classroom, particularly if a teacher tries to talk over chatter, but a soft, low-pitched voice is restful and calming. The "soft reprimand" is also effective in a similar way. Our normal tendency is to raise our voices to correct a student's behavior but research suggests that students respond to **lowered** voice volumes better than to raised voices--in part because of the unexpected change and in part because soft reprimands are more private and tend not to invite loud protestations, denials, or retorts. It is especially important to model super-quiet voice levels when monitoring student work by circulating to individuals.

5. The Cueing Principle

Behavioral psychology has also given us new insights into the nature and effectiveness of cues--generally, non-verbal reminders about behavioral expectations--in strengthening discipline practices. Of course, good teachers have always known that cues improve discipline. The teacher who raises his hand for silence, flips the light switch to get attention, points to a group of gigglers and then presses her finger to her lips in the classic "sh-sh-sh" sign is reminding students of certain rules, procedures, or expectations.

Some students (whether by choice or insensitive perception) seem oblivious to the cues that are built into the classroom--the bell ringing to signal the beginning of class, for example--or that a teacher uses intuitively or naturally--the teacher putting hands on hips to signal she is waiting for attention, for example. In this situation, a teacher should (1) examine the cues he uses, (2) establish stronger, more explicit variations of the cues, (3) teach the cues to the students in a direct fashion, (4) pair the new cue with a verbal explanation of it while using it. A brief

116

example may help to clarify this approach. Let's take the teacher who stands with hands on hips waiting for attention. She might first conclude that the students do not grasp the significance of the cue. In the second place, she might decide to combine the cue with movement toward the class and a clearing of the throat. In the third place, she could explain to the students that these cues are designed to let them know that she is waiting for attention. Lastly, she can, at the next opportunity, use the non-verbal cues while saying, "As you can see, I am waiting for your attention, class."

A creative teacher--especially one who enjoys the performing aspects of teaching--can develop a host of novel cues employing proximity, facial expressions, gestures, and objects (bells, lights, "clickers") to supplement **verbal** cues ("OK, boys and girls, in ten seconds you will need your protractors") that keep the behavioral expectations flowing from teacher to student and vice versa. One teacher I know teaches his students new ways to cue **him**. Instead of asking them to raise their hands to be recognized to answer a question, he will say, "If you know the answer, put your head on your desk" (when they are too restless), or "If you know the answer, stand up" (if they need to stretch), or "If you know the answer, pull on your right ear lobe" (if they need to be amused). Such experimentation with cueing techniques helps kids learn to be more sensitive to this approach to communication. Effective communication is essential to effective discipline.

6. The Environmental Control Principle

There are many things a teacher cannot control in a student's background, e.g., whether or not he had breakfast, the parents' child-rearing practices, or handicapping conditions. But the environmental control principle says that a wise teacher uses the classroom environment to its maximum to improve both learning and behavior. In terms of altering the environment, a teacher may enrich, impoverish, restrict, enlarge, simplify, or systematize. Let us look at a couple of opposing alterations that can improve discipline.

Often classroom management is a problem because students are bored, apathetic, uninterested, and unmotivated. In such a situation, the teacher needs to enrich the environment to improve motivation, attention, and involvement. Here the teacher might give consideration to learning centers, bulletin boards, music,

117

and other audio-visual techniques to provide a variety
of stimuli. Lessons could begin with inductive techniques derived from objects. "Here is a replica of a
kitchen implement used by ancient Egyptian housewives,
class. What uses could it be put to then? Now?"
Whenever a teacher enriches the environment, she consciously adds to and varies the environment for an educational process. Enrichment done well motivates and
motivated students engage in learning rather than misbehavior.

On the other hand, classroom management is often a
problem because students are over-stimulated by the environment. In some classes students are easily dis-
tracted, tend toward hyperactivity, and have short attention spans. In this situation the teacher may need
to **impoverish** the environment to improve control and
student attention. If a teacher tries to be enthusiastic and motivating, the result is often disastrous
as the additional stimuli only raises the kinetic energy level in the room--like turning up the flame under a
bubbling cauldron. Instead, the teacher should attempt
to lower the energy level and stimuli by darkening the
room, using carpets, removing distracting materials and
diversions, scheduling quiet times and quiet corners,
and using focusing techniques such as filmstrips and
directed study lessons. Finally, the teacher himself
should be an exemplary model of controlled activity,
concentration, and subdued behavior--especially in
terms of voice volume, dress, and movement. Such
"impoverishing" of the environment turns down the
flame under the cauldron of student activity.

7. The "Low Profile" Intervention Principle

This principle also follows from some of the pio-
neering research in group management by Jacob Kounin
but is enjoying the renewed attention in current research. The concept here is that the teacher herself
should manage student behavior as discreetly, unobtru-
sively, and smoothly as possible--avoiding direct confrontations and public encounters with disruptive students. The teacher needs to anticipate behavior problems and nip problems in-the-bud without constant
ordering and commanding (high profile interventions).
In a sense, all of the principles discussed so far are
low intervention techniques.

A particularly effective approach during whole
class instruction is to drop a name of a student whose

attention is wandering into the middle of an instructional sentence: "We need to remember, Clarence, Columbus was one of several discoverers of America." (Note: I once used this technique only to find on a later quiz that the students thought that Clarence Columbus came to America!) The teacher may "drop" several names of students during a presentation but should do so almost casually with no hint of reprisal and no pause for reply. Another low intervention technique is to move close to students who are beginning to get off task so that the teacher's proximity curtails misbehavior or inattention. Such "overlapping" of teacher behaviors --e.g., moving to trouble spots while conducting the lesson--becomes almost automatic with practice and can be enhanced by additional non-verbal actions, such as touching a student on the shoulder or quietly opening the student's book to the proper page.

8. The Assertive Discipline Principle

This principle, made popular by Lee Canter, calls for higher profile, non-hostile interventions that are effective in communicating a teacher's wants and needs for better discipline. Actually, assertive discipline is only a common sense combination of behavioral psychology (praise) and traditional authoritarianism (limit setting). The teacher needs first of all to identify specific roadblocks to discipline, roadblocks that are generally the consequence of a teacher's low expectations of student behavior. Teachers should start from a position of confidence that students can behave appropriately and that no child has the right to violate the rights of other students to learn and the teachers to teach. Next, the assertive teacher communicates expectations to students through clear rules that are carefully explained to students. Finally, the teacher consistently follows through with systematic consequences and with verbal and non-verbal limits so that students know that the teacher means what she says.

Perhaps the keys to the assertive discipline principle are best found in the teacher's **attitude** and **actions**. The attitude of the teacher must be one of confidence, competence, and caring. Assertive teachers know that students can behave, follow rules, and learn and these teachers communicate these positive expectations in a business-like, no-nonsense, firm manner. In terms of actions, they never threaten, plead, or shout; rather, they promise, request, and use assertion messages. A cardinal rule is, as Canter says,

119

"Thou shalt not make a demand thou art not prepared to follow through upon."

Specific techniques that follow from this principle of management include: (1) rules that are clear and specific; (2) consequences that are sequenced from mild to severe (Canter suggests **one** set of consequences that is systematically and consistently applied when <u>any</u> rule is broken); (3) verbal limit setting through requests, hints, and demands; (4) non-verbal communications--eye contact, proximity, touch, gestures--that leave no doubt about what is required of whom; (5) "broken record" confrontations with students (repeating requests for compliance several times so that students know the teacher cannot be diverted nor ignored). These techniques, along with positive consequences for following rules and requests, provide clear evidence to students that the teacher knows what he wants and needs in the area of student behavior and that students' responses will generate positive or negative consequences for **them**.

9. The I-Message Principle

Both the assertive discipline approach of Lee Canter and the humanistic discipline approach of Haim Ginott and Thomas Gordon (of **TET** fame) rely on clear communication between teachers and students, and both approaches advocate the use of I-messages by teachers. Because assertive discipline and humanistic discipline operate on entirely different premises, the I-message principle takes two forms.

A teacher may communicate a particular demand, want, or need in order to be more assertive. This works particularly well for refocusing a group or individual and is a regular part of the assertive teacher's broken record technique. Here the teacher uses "I want you to..." or "I need you to..." before giving a specific request: "...start working on the math assignment" or "...listen to my directions for the essay." Such I-message assertions are more effective than "you stop..." types of messages which focus on confrontations ("you") and on past infractions ("stop"). An assertive I-message tells students exactly what the teacher wants and expects the student to **do**.

From the humanistic perspective, I-messages enable a teacher to communicate his or her **feelings** so that students can understand more clearly the effect their behavior has on the teacher. According to Gordon, an

120

I-message has three elements: (1) the description of the students' behavior ("When you leave our room in a mess"); (2) the effect of that behavior on the teacher ("I have to lose instructional time cleaning up"); (3) the feeling that causes the teacher ("and this frustrates me"). Such messages encourage students voluntarily to change their misbehavior. Both forms of the I-message have their place in the repertoire of the effective classroom manager.

10. The Positive Reinforcement Principle

One of the best known principles of classroom management from the behaviorists is the "catch 'em being good" principle of positive reinforcement. The principle tells the teacher that punishment not only does not work (except temporarily) in changing behavior but it can provide attention to negative behavior and actually increase undesirable student behavior. A combination of (1) ignoring minor misbehavior and (2) identifying and praising good behavior will have better long-range effects on classroom discipline than punishment. In practice this is harder to do than one might think and although teachers understand the principle, research shows that most teachers are less than skillful in **applying** the positive reinforcement principle to improve behavior. But there are several specific application techniques a teacher can use to develop better discipline.

One practice a teacher can employ is positive rules and expectations. Once students know the rule is "Raise your hand for permission to talk" rather than "Do not call out if you have not been recognized," the teacher can praise students who follow the positive rule instead of punishing people for breaking the negative rule. "Thank you for raising your hand, Freddy; you have certainly followed our rule to the letter." Praise, a major technique for positive reinforcement, should be sincere, personalized, descriptive, and focused on the **acts** of students rather than their character or personality. Teachers can set up positive expectations by saying, "Let's see how quickly we can distribute the art supplies," and follow this with praise directed at individuals or groups conforming to the expectation: "The group in the back has set up all of the paints and is ready to begin." A teacher has to **look** for good behavior and **practice** describing it in a complimentary fashion.

There are a host of non-verbal reinforcers (nods, smiles, touch), activity reinforcers (games, field trips, free time), and concrete or token reinforcers (candy, charts, check marks) that a teacher can apply as a reward for good behavior. For example, a teacher could have a special place on the board to put up names of "super citizens"--students who have made some contribution to the welfare of the class that day. Such students could be the first to go to lunch the next day. A teacher might tell a restless class that she is setting an egg timer for somewhere between one and three minutes when the students have been directed to work quietly. If it goes off when they are quiet (catching them being good), the class receives a reward--such as some free time at the end of the period. The teacher should at **first** set the timer for a short period of time so that the class is almost bound to be on task. As their habits and concentration improve, the time should be lengthened but should not be predictable.

There is much more to establishing good discipline than most teachers believe. Indeed, these few principles and the "tricks of the trade" they generate are but one aspect of the art of discipline. In the final analysis, classroom control of student behavior deals primarily (but necessarily) with the symptoms of misbehavior, and the manifestations of more fundamental dynamics of behavior: hostility, frustration, discouragement, and apathy. Control is important but it is not enough. Ultimately, a teacher's discipline will depend on long term relationships with children, effective instructional practices, an ability to convince students that school is important. School is important when teachers reach students with meaningful lessons and a professional commitment that says "I care about you; I know you can behave; I want to help you be a **better** you."

THE DISCIPLINE PRIMER SELF-EVALUATION QUIZ

Check your discipline practices for classroom control by rating your own practices below. Add your totals in each column. Score yourself as follows: 90-100, excellent; 80-90, good; 70-80, fair; below 70, poor.

	4 pt. Usually	2 pt. Sometimes	0 pt. Never
1. I get students' attention before giving instruction(s).			
2. I wait for students to attend rather than talk over chatter.			
3. I quickly get students on task.			
4. I give clear and specific directions.			
5. I set explicit time limits for task completion.			
6. I circulate among students at work.			
7. I hold private conferences/ conversations during class.			
8. I model courtesy and politeness.			
9. I model quiet by using a low volume voice.			
10. I use the "soft reprimand" rather than raising my voice.			
11. I use a variety of cues to remind students of expected behavior.			
12. I teach students my cues.			
13. I enrich my classroom to improve motivation.			
14. I impoverish my class to improve attention.			
15. I am aware of the effects of my dress, voice, and movement on student behavior.			
16. I use student names as low profile correctors of inattention.			
17. I use proximity to improve classroom control.			

	4 pt. Usually	2 pt. Sometimes	0 pt. Never
18. I communicate positive expectations of good behavior to my class.			
19. I have clear, specific rules that I teach my students.			
20. I refuse to threaten or plead with students.			
21. I consistently follow through with consequences to enforce rules.			
22. I use I-messages assertively to tell students what I want them to do.			
23. I use I-messages humanistically to communicate my feelings.			
24. I praise behaviors I like with specific, personal praise statements.			
25. I use non-verbal, social, and activity reinforcers.			

A PRIMER ON MOTIVATION:
PRINCIPLES OLD AND NEW

What does a teacher need to do to motivate today's students to learn? Fifty years ago the topic of motivation was virtually ignored in teacher education programs. Teachers of that day were told to "have a good lesson plan," "be enthusiastic," and "use grades and prizes" to stimulate interest.

Later, the behaviorists developed and promoted some techniques of "extrinsic motivation" that were derived from reinforcement theory. Many of these techniques found their way into schools in the form of behavior modification programs, most notably in special education classes. Later still, humanistic educators and psychologists--Carl Rogers, Abraham Maslow, Rudolf Dreikurs, and others--told teachers to focus on "intrinsic motivation": developing self-concept, meeting individual needs, and encouraging student progress.

Today we are asked to improve classroom climate, mediate transactions, and invite school success. The contemporary teacher is likely to be confused and not a little daunted by the number of motivational techniques recommended for the classroom.

And it is not just that we have more theories now, either; we also ascribe more importance to them. The newfound interest in teacher and school effectiveness, the public concern for higher achievement test scores, and the social problems--discipline, drugs, dropouts-- of both the community and the school all contribute to new demands that teachers and their classrooms be more motivating. How can schools expect higher productivity and achievement unless students **somehow** become more interested in and committed to their own educational improvement? This is the essential challenge of instructional motivation, and the challenge is one that confronts the overburdened classroom teacher daily. So, what's a teacher to do?

Motivation is complex and controversial, but it is also a crucial element in instructional success. Why a student will "move" toward instructional goals and how to maximize that movement are questions that arise in every classroom in every school and are resolved-- for good or ill--by individual teachers. Nonetheless, there appears to be an emerging set of principles to guide teacher behaviors related to effective instruc-

125

tional motivation. Of course, principles are no better
than the teachers who put them into practice, but I
present the following five principles as an eclectic
combination of techniques--traditional and modern,
practical and theoretical, pedagogical and psycholo-
gical--that teachers **can** use to produce better motivation. Although in reality these principles are closely
connected, even interrelated, each focuses on a given
aspect of the teacher's role as motivator.

1. The Inviting Success Principle

This motivational principle, named by William Purkey, expresses a humanistic notion that students behave
in accordance with a teacher's **perception** of their
ability. An invitation, says Purkey in **Inviting School
Success,** "is a summary description of messages--verbal
and nonverbal, formal and informal--continuously trans-
mitted to students with the intention of informing them
that they are responsible, able, and valuable."[1]   A
major premise from which this view of motivation is derived is that positive self-concept is the key to student motivation to learn.

The principle of inviting success is a foundation
for several of the other principles of motivation listed below, but it is of special value as the expression
of an attitude that effective motivators demonstrate in
their relationships with children--an attitude that
says in word and deed, "I care about you, I trust you,
I know you are somebody, I know you can learn."   How
much faith do you have in your students?   Can you
develop and demonstrate more?

More specifically, a teacher should examine words
and actions that might be obstacles to motivation.   Do
you let previous records, horror stories from other
teachers, or ability grouping influence your confidence
in your students' capacity to learn?   Do you slip into
sarcasm or ridicule?   Do you find yourself continually
using such negative terms as "no," "stop," and "don't"?
The principle of inviting success asks you to change
your perceptions and attitude so that you can bid students to become the trustworthy, capable human beings
you **know** they can be.

Invitational techniques include being explicit in
sending invitations, talking directly to students and
using their names frequently, giving all students your
attention and time, reserving time for one-on-one contact with students, listening with care and respect,

providing more opportunities for students to talk and participate in class, developing class spirit, letting students know they are missed, using student experts whenever possible, and promoting cooperation.

2. The Cooperative Learning Principle

Competition has long been honored and practiced as a means of motivating learning by way of games, contests, incentives, and rewards. But teachers can also motivate students by cooperative strategies. Cooperation can often reach those youngsters who lose in competitions. Indeed, our public schools may have inadvertently created a large number of "losers" by overemphasizing competition. Students who make no teams, win no prizes, and earn no rewards for superior performance may conclude that they have few reasons for continued effort in the classroom. At the very least, schools should consider ways of balancing the competitive ethos--which the "excellence movement" is likely to exacerbate--with cooperative activities designed to enhance the motivation of noncompetitive students.

At the Cooperative Learning Center at the University of Minnesota, David Johnson, Roger Johnson, and their colleagues have developed a variety of cooperative learning strategies described in such books as **Learning Together and Alone, Joining Together,** and **Circles of Learning.**[2] These researchers contend that "teachers must be prepared to teach needed collaborative skills in order for cooperative learning to be productive."[3] Cooperative learning requires that teachers group students heterogeneously and structure goals to promote positive interdependence of members; teachers must promote shared responsibility for leadership **and** learning; they must directly teach such social skills as leadership behavior, communication, and conflict management; and they must analyze and evaluate for the groups of students the process being used to solve problems and share work.

This motivational principle works because it promotes higher levels of self-esteem while also promoting "belongingness." The teacher needs to set clear goals, explain the criteria for success, structure the group for individual (as well as group) accountability, monitor the process and intervene when necessary, and provide directions for the task. In addition to the product of the group's work, the teacher must pay attention to the process, especially by allowing groups to evaluate their own effectiveness. When students learn the joy of working productively together toward common goals, motivation inevitably improves.

3. The High Expectations Principle

Much of the research on school effectiveness points to the importance of high expectations for students. The principle of inviting success depends on high expectations, and the cooperative learning principle suggests that teachers should expect students to accomplish important affective learning while meeting academic goals. But the principle of high expectations is more far-reaching. It addresses the importance of self-fulfilling prophecies and of teacher behaviors that communicate high expectations.

Sad to say, negative expectations abound in classrooms, especially in classrooms filled with low-achieving students. Current research shows that teachers generally seat low-ability students farther away from themselves, call on low-ability students less often, pay less attention to low-ability students, give low-ability students less time and fewer clues for answering questions, criticize wrong answers from low-ability students more often and praise their correct responses less often, and interrupt the performance of low-ability students more often. Such behaviors communicate lower expectations, less tolerance, and even less affection for low-ability students than for their high-ability classmates. Consequently, the students create negative self-fulfilling prophecies that lead them to become less confident, more passive or more disruptive, and less motivated to work up to their capacity.

The first step in helping **all** students to meet high expectations is to analyze seating assignments, interaction patterns, and teaching practices to identify and correct any negative behaviors. Next, a teacher might examine classroom rules. Do they include long lists (more than five) of negative behaviors that are not allowed? Or do they focus on positive behaviors that are expected? Negative rules convey implicitly the teacher's assumption that, say, fighting, cheating, talking, destroying property, and cursing **will** occur if not prohibited. Positive rules--"walk quietly in the halls," "keep your work space clean," and so on --convey **positive** expectations.

In the academic area teachers can direct students toward future success. Instead of criticizing mistakes, look for what is good in a student's work. To help students see the potential for growth, use positive suggestions, such as "I expect that, with practice, your multiplication will improve each day."

Teachers must also set clear and explicit goals for student learning each day. These goals should be challenging but not **too** difficult. Teachers should communicate these goals as expectations and let students know that--though the work ahead may be difficult--they **can** achieve.

4. The Set Induction Principle

This principle relates to teacher behaviors designed to include "readiness to learn" in students. Instructional motivation depends on a teacher's skill in getting students to attend to the objectives, skills, knowledge, and values that constitute any given lesson. The old saying goes, "You can lead a horse to water, but you can't make him drink." Motivation by set induction says, "Yes, but you can put salt in the oats!" Set induction can be accomplished by a variety of "focusing events" or "advance organizers" (to borrow David Ausubel's term). The idea is to prepare students for learning by grabbing their attention with an activity that is arresting and relevant (to the lesson **and** to the students' experience).

Consider a few specific techniques. A teacher can begin a lesson with a perplexing question that leaves students intrigued. For example, "If rain falls out of clouds, why don't clouds fall too?" Or (to set up a lesson in grammar), "What would happen if we eliminated all verbs from the English language?" Such questions can establish a state of disequilibrium, a state of tension that motivates students to resolve a problem or dilemma. Whenever we confront students with questions or problems that depart from their experience, we motivate them to relieve the disequilibrium.

Another application of this principle can be found in special objects and activities that focus students on the concepts to be studied. For example, a teacher might hold up a knotted rope before beginning a lesson on the umbilical cord or a faded rose before discussing the theme of "lost beauty." Such objects can be stimuli for questions or brainstorming. Or a teacher could ask students to speculate on why a mechanical bird balanced on the edge of a glass of water magically dips to "drink" from the glass from time to time; all hypo-

129

theses could be recorded on the board.

More elaborate applications of set induction could include longer activities that start where the students are, but connect to the lesson content. To motivate students for a lesson on slavery before the Civil War, a teacher might begin to discriminate against the blue-eyed (or short or left-handed) children in the class, requiring them to do extra homework, sit in the back of the room, be dismissed last, and so on. Or, in preparation for a lesson on the Plains Indians, a teacher might show a slide depicting an Indian and give students one minute to observe everything they can. Afterward, the teacher could ask whether the Indian had a weapon or what markings were on the Indian's left arm. Inference questions could follow, such as "Was the Indian angry? How do you know? What caused him to be angry?" This in turn could lead to reading a chapter in a history book for the purpose of generating additional answers to these questions. Set induction provides structure, direction, and relevance that together pique curiosity and promote motivation to learn.

5. The Interaction Principle

How can a teacher ask questions and handle responses in ways that increase involvement, participation, interest, and thinking? Teachers who are good motivators know that their interactions and transactions with students are central to a successful lesson. Such teachers enjoy classroom discussion, use humor, draw on personal experiences (theirs and the students'), keep open minds, invite students to teach the teacher, keep a lively pace, and demonstrate genuine enthusiasm. But beyond these general behaviors, they also give special attention to the kinds of questions they ask students and the kinds of strategies they employ when students answer (or don't answer) a question.

Consider questioning techniques. For an invitational teacher, the basic purpose of questioning is to give students every opportunity possible to show what they know, think, and value. Students quickly lose interest when they discover that questions are designed to find out what they do **not** know and call for convergent responses that will be immediately judged. Motivating questions usually involve little risk for the responders and allow many acceptable answers. Some questions--such as "Let's see who forgot to read the homework assignment. Joe, can you define a prime number?"--tend to be high risk, convergent, and threatening. On the other hand, a question such as "I know you found the assignment on prime numbers interesting and difficult. I wonder if anyone can give us one example of a prime number--Joe?" has a much better chance of motivating a response.

One key to handling student responses successfully is "wait time." A teacher who thoughtfully waits three to five seconds (the average wait time is about **one** second) can expect more answers, longer answers, and better-reasoned answers. Another valuable technique is to ask some questions that even the teacher cannot answer. (It is ironic that teachers who **know** answers ask questions of students who do not.) When possible, suspend judgment on responses by securing several responses before commenting or by saying, "Tell me more about that." Always judging responses and giving too much praise--especially in higher-ability classes--have negative effects on interaction and the response rate. Using questions as a means of increasing motivation requires teachers to develop the skills of divergent and higher-order questioning and the skills of redirecting and suspending judgment.

There is more to good motivation than most teachers believe. Indeed, these few principles and tricks of the trade are but one part of the art of instructional motivation. Teachers can learn how to personalize instruction (using names more frequently, greeting students as they enter the room, using personal examples as a basis for learning); they can learn how to use small-group instruction more effectively, how to capitalize on what students already know, how to end every lesson on a positive note, how to individualize better and provide greater choice, how to use unfinished activity, and how to build interest in the curriculum itself. All of these principles, strategies, and techniques have a place in the repertoire of a teacher who has learned to motivate students for success. Effective teachers use their motivational skills to develop a positive climate that nurtures the educational growth of children. Are **you** skilled in the basics of instructional motivation?

NOTES

[1]William Purkey, **Inviting School Success: A Self-Concept Approach to Teaching and Learning** (Belmont, Calif.: Wadsworth, 1978), p. 3.

[2]David W. Johnson and Roger T. Johnson, **Learning Together and Alone: Cooperation, Competition, and Individualization** (Englewood, Cliffs, N. J.: Prentice-Hall, 1975); idem, **Joining Together: Group Theory and Group Skills** (Englewood Cliffs, N. J.: Prentice-Hall, 1982); and David W. Johnson, Roger T. Johnson, Edith Johnson Holubec, and Patricia Roy, **Circles of Learning: Cooperation in the Classroom** (Alexandria, Va.: Association for Supervision and Curriculum Development, 1984).

[3]Johnson et al., p. v.

HOW GOOD A MOTIVATOR ARE YOU?

Check your motivational practices by rating yourself on the questions below. Add your totals in each column. Score yourself as follows: 90-100, excellent; 80-90, good; 70-80, fair; below 70, poor.

	Usu-ally (4 pt)	Some-times (2 pt)	Never (0 pt)
1. I believe my students are competent & trustworthy.			
2. I avoid labeling students.			
3. I avoid sarcasm, put-downs, and ridicule of students.			
4. I send explicit invitations to succeed.			
5. I listen to what my students really say.			
6. I let students know they are missed.			
7. I make good use of student experts in the class.			
8. I use heterogeneous groups to build interdependence.			
9. I teach leadership and communicate skills.			
10. I avoid overemphasis on competition, rewards, and winning.			
11. I help groups evaluate their effectiveness in group process.			
12. I give equal time, atten-tion, and support to low-ability students.			
13. I communicate high expec-tations to my students.			
14. I focus on future success rather than past failures.			
15. I look for what is positive in student work & behavior.			
16. I set and communicate clear goals for instruction.			
17. I use well-designed, thought-provoking questions to stimulate readiness.			

	Usu-ally (4 pt)	Some-times (2 pt)	Never (0 pt)
18. I use objects as "focusing events" to stimulate interest.			
19. I use brainstorming to stimulate interest before beginning a lesson.			
20. I use set induction acti-vities that connect a present experience to a lesson concept.			
21. I ask low-risk, open-ended questions.			
22. I wait three to five minutes after asking a divergent question.			
23. I suspend judgment and re-direct a question to get multiple responses.			
24. I paraphrase and clarify responses instead of judging and praising.			
25. I personalize learning.			

ABOUT THE AUTHOR

THOMAS R. McDANIEL, a native of Herndon, Virginia, is Charles A. Dana Professor of Education, Director of Graduate Education Studies, and Interim Dean at Converse College, Spartanburg, South Carolina. He received his undergraduate training at Hampden-Sydney College where he graduated **magna cum laude** with majors in English and psychology. He earned the MAT (English), MLA (Humanities), and Ph.D. (Education) from The Johns Hopkins University, specializing in administration and philosophy in his doctoral work. Prior to his appointment at Converse in 1971, he taught English and Latin in public and private schools and served for seven years as Assistant and Associate Director of the MAT program, Supervisor of Interns, and Instructor in Micro-teaching at Johns Hopkins. His honors include Phi Beta Kappa, Omicron Delta Kappa, Psi Chi, Gamma Sigma, Sigma Upsilon, Alpha Psi Omega, Eta Sigma Phi, Pi Gamma Mu, Phi Sigma Pi, and Who's Who Among Students in American Universities and Colleges. Professor McDaniel has served on the Spartanburg County Board of Education (Chairman), The South Carolina Society for the Study of the Foundations of Education (President), the Board of Directors of The Charles Lea Center (Chairman), and on many other boards and committees. Professional journals have published over one hundred of his articles, essays, and reviews, and his work has been included in such anthologies as **The Cream of the Kappan 1956-81**, and **Kaleidoscope: Readings in Education.** He has also written a textbook chapter for **The Reality of Teaching** (Kendall/Hunt) and has given dozens of workshops and speeches locally and nationally on such topics as school law and school discipline. University Press of America published his texts **The Teacher's Profession** in 1982 and **The Teacher's Dilemma** in 1983. He has also edited **Public Education in South Carolina**, published by Edwards Brothers in 1984. Dr. McDaniel resides in Spartanburg with his wife, Nan, and his children, Robb and Katy.